ARACHNOMANIA

The General Care and Maintenance of

Tarantulas and Scorpions

by

Philippe de Vosjoli

P9-DMK-479

Table of Contents

Introduction

It's not arachnophobia that concerns me; it's arachnomania. I can feel it. It's coming upon us. A nightmare come true, giant spiders at every turn..
                              - Late twentieth century visionary. Name withheld by request.

Arachnomania: An excitement or craze associated with the keeping of arachnids: tarantulas, scorpions and the like.

Arachnoculture: The interdisciplinary field concerned with the husbandry and propagation of arachnids.

Arachnoculturist: An individual involved in the husbandry and propagation of arachnids.

In recent years, there has been an increasing interest in the keeping of land invertebrates in the United States. Tarantulas, scorpions and millipedes are now standard fare in the pet trade. Unusual appearance, aesthetic appeal, suitability for display in a naturalistic terrarium, and ease of maintenance are some of the many factors which have led to the rise of popularity of these invertebrates.

One of the newer phenomena in the trade has been the emergence of specialist collectors willing to pay high prices for what has usually been thought of as low price-range animals. Some of the tarantulas today may fetch as much as $200.00. When these trends become apparent, there usually is financial motivation to develop husbandry and captive-breeding methods which eventually will result in the commercial production of the more desirable species. One of the aspects that make tarantulas worthwhile as an investment is that unlike most terrestrial arthropods, they are relatively long-lived with life-spans usually ranging from six to twenty years or more. As display animals, they are relatively hardy and easy to maintain. From a breeder/investor point of view, they tend to be productive breeders often laying between 50 and 500 (sometimes more) eggs per breeding. With spiderlings being bought by collectors at prices ranging from $10.00 to $75.00, investors are looking at the possibility of captive breeding as a source of supplemental income which can be developed in a relatively small space and with a relatively small investment.

In terms of the dynamics of the pet market in the U.S., all the indications are that spiders, scorpions and other land arthropods are about to become established as a new field in the pet trade. Arachnomania is looming over the horizon. Its companion arachnoculture, is following suit.

To date, the handful of books available in the U.S. have focused on the popular, but no longer readily available, Mexican red-leg tarantula. The goal of this book is to present an overview of methods for the husbandry of a variety of tarantulas and representatives of scorpions as well. Another goal is to present a profile of the many new species which are appearing on the American pet market. The author acknowledges the limitations of this book particularly with regards to the life history information that would be interesting to prospective breeders. This is a preliminary work on a subject which must be still be considered in its infancy. In time, as we all learn more about these fascinating animals, additional updated works will follow.

Part One
Tarantulas

The Mexican red-leg tarantula (*Euathlus smithi*), one of the most attractive and popular of the tarantulas. This is a four year old captive-raised individual.

General Information

GUIDELINES FOR THE RESPONSIBLE KEEPING OF TARANTULAS

It is critical that all pet owners act in a responsible manner with regards to the keeping of their pets if they wish to continue to enjoy and practice their avocation without restrictive legislation and regulations. Irresponsible pet keeping threatens the rights of all of us who need to have interaction with animals as an intrinsic part of our lives. The following are guidelines for the responsible keeping of tarantulas:

1. Tarantulas should be kept in secure enclosures that preclude the possibility of escape. Such enclosures should have a screw-on type lid or snap on cover or a sliding cover or a framed cover. Taped plastic boxes are also suitable.

2. Tarantulas should not be kept by minors without parental consent to assume responsibility for proper housing, maintenance and supervision in the course of maintenance. As a general rule, children should not be allowed to handle tarantulas.

3. Unwanted tarantulas should never be intentionally released.

4. No tarantulas should ever be displayed openly in public outside of a proper setting for such displays such as pet shows or educational displays.

CHANGING PROFILES OF THE TARANTULA MARKET

At one time, the most widely sold of all tarantulas was the Mexican red-leg tarantula *(Euathlus smithi)*, a large, heavy bodied and attractive tarantula which became very popular because of its beauty, hardiness and docility. Today, this species is protected and seldom available. Other popular species which were once regularly imported, included the Mexican painted or orange-knee tarantula *(Euathlus emilia)*, Haitian tarantula *(Phormictopus cancerides)* and various Central American species (i.e., *Euathlus albopilosa, E. vagans*) which are not readily available at the time of writing.

The availability of tarantulas is controlled and limited by the changing wildlife laws of respective countries. If a country becomes open to animal exportation, then native tarantulas may be exported. If a country closes its animal exports then tarantulas usually (but not always because the laws are not always applied to invertebrates) stop being exported. The result of all this is a changing tarantula market. Because of the fast growing interest in keeping large spiders, animal importers in general are making more efforts to obtain various tarantula species and a greater variety is now available than ever before.

There is also an increased interest in the captive breeding of the more popular and expensive tarantulas to supply the steady demand for these species. To date, most captive-breeding efforts have been in Europe. We are seeing increasing numbers of imported captive-born and, occasionally, captive-raised animals becoming available on dealers' price lists. Most of the tarantulas sold in the U.S today are being offered by specialized dealers, usually amphibian and reptile specialists. The large number of imported species available and the increasing numbers of captive-produced animals has radically changed today's tarantula market. In the future, American hobbyists are expected to become more interested in the captive-breeding of these animals and regular availability of many of the most desirable species can be anticipated.

WHAT ARE TARANTULAS?

The popular name tarantula is now generally accepted by hobbyists to designate the approximately 800 species of large primitive spiders in the family Theraphosidae, one of several families in the suborder Orthognatha (formerly Mygalomorpha). For the sake of presenting the reader with a profile of the Theraphosidae, the following is an overview of the subfamilies and groups (from Raven 1985 and from Smith 1990):

OLD WORLD

SUBFAMILY	GROUPS	POPULAR GENERA
AFRICA		
Eumenophorinae		*Citharischius, Heterscodra*
		Stromatopelma
Harpactirinae		*Ceratogyrus, Pterinochilus*
Ischnocolinae		
Selenogyrinae		New family proposed by Andrew Smith.
MIDDLE EAST		
Ischnocolinae		
INDIA/FAR EAST/ORIENTAL REGION		
Ornithoctoninae		*Haplopelma*
Selenocosmiinae		
	a) Selenocosmieae	*Selenocosmia*
	b) Poecilotheriae	*Poecilotheria*
Thrigmipoeinae		

NEW WORLD

SUBFAMILY	GROUPS	POPULAR GENERA
Aviculariina		*Avicularia, Psalmopoeus*
Theraphosinae.		
	a)Grammostoleae	*Euathlus, Grammostola, Rhechosticta*
	b)Theraphoseae	*Lasiodora, Megaphobema, Pamphobeteus, Theraphosa*
Acanthopelma		
Spelopelma		

Note: The systematics of the Theraphosidae has undergone considerable changes in recent years; new research in this area will undoubtedly result in additional changes. Other works are scheduled to be published on this subject in the not too distant future. The above material is presented to the reader so that he or she can make some sense out of the various tarantula species offered in the trade and is in no way intended to state a position on the systematics of the Theraphosidae.

For information on the various species of tarantulas and their systematics, the hobbyist will find the following to be useful references:

Raven, R. 1985. The Spider Infraorder Mygalamorphae (Araneae): Cladistics and Systematics. Bull. Amer. Mus. Nat. Hist. Vol 182 no 1 pp 1-180. This is a primary reference on the current systematics of the Theraphosid spiders.

Schmidt, Gunther. 1989. Vogelspinnen. published in Germany by Bluchel & Philler Verlag. Minden. 55 color photos, 126 pp. This book is available through some specialized dealers in the U.S. It is written in German, but presents valuable information on systematics as well as detailed lists of the various species and their distribution.

Smith, A.M. 1990. Baboon spiders. Tarantulas of Africa and the Middle East. Fitzgerald Publishing, London. Numerous diagrams, a small number of black and white photos in a 142 page spiral bound notebook format. This is the first of three volumes in this set by Smith to be published on tarantulas. The other two volumes will be:
Vol 2. Earth Tigers. The Theraphosidae of The Far East.
Vol 3. Tarantulas. The Theraphosidae of North and South America.
The format of the first book focuses on presenting no-nonsense keys to identification. It also presents valuable notes on distribution, habitat and occasionally breeding, as well as anthropological information. This book is expensive, but will

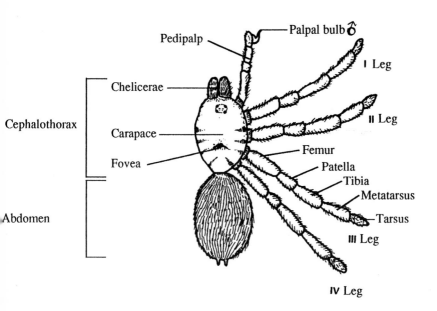

Dorsal view of a tarantula. Illustration by Russ Gurley.

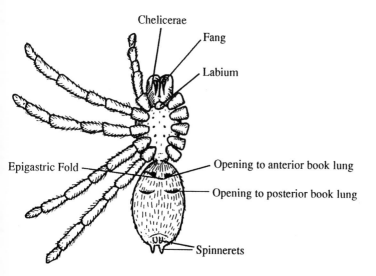

Ventral view of a tarantula. Illustration by Russ Gurley.

prove invaluable to serious hobbyists wishing to learn something about the taxonomic methods and tools involved in the study of tarantulas. As a guide to tarantulas of Africa and the Middle East, there is no better one on the market available to the hobbyist.

Names of Popular Tarantulas

Asian black velvet - *Haplopelma minax*
Chilean flame tarantula - *Grammostola spatulata*
Chilean rose tarantula - *Grammostola gala*
Curly-haired tarantula - *Euathlus albopilosa*
Goliath bird-eater - *Theraphosa leblondi*
Indian ornamental rainforest tarantula - *Poecilotheria regalis*
King baboon spider - *Citharischius crawshayi*
Mexican red-leg tarantula - *Euathlus smithi*
Orange-knee or painted tarantula - *Euathlus emilia*
Pink-toed tarantula - *Avicularia avicularia*
Red-rump tarantula - *Euathlus vagans*
Striped-knee or zebra tarantula - *Rhechosticta seemanni*
Starburst baboon spider - *Pterinochilus murinus*
Trinidad chevron tree spider - *Psalmopoeus cambridgei*

SEXING

Sexing of tarantulas becomes possible once they reach sexual maturity. At that time, males will emerge from their last molt bearing small shiny structures called palpal bulbs and the associated spine-like processes called emboli (one embolus per palpal bulb used for transfer of sperm to females) on the underside of the ends of the pedipalps. Only close observation will allow one to readily notice these structures. In many tarantulas species (but not all), the most obvious secondary sexual characteristics in males following their last molt will be the presence of tibial spurs (in most species, hook-like structures at the end of the tibias, in others, mounds of smaller spines at the ends of the tibias) on the first set of legs.

Prior to the adult molt, an educated guess can be made about males, particularly in groups of captive-raised spiderlings either by their comparatively smaller body size, or by their more slender appearing abdomens. In many species, males generally give the impression of being more spindly.

Females are generally more heavy-bodied than males and in many species tend to be larger. The best indication of a female reaching maturity is breeding behavior following introduction of a male and, eventually, laying of eggs and the formation of an egg sac.

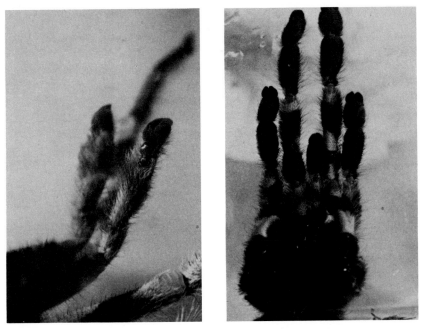

The most reliable way to sex tarantulas is to look for palpal bulbs and the associated spine-like emboli on the underside of the ends (tarsi) of the pedipalps. A palpal bulb is clearly visible on the underside of the pedipalp in this male ornamental rainforest tarantula (left). For the sake of comparison, a female is shown on the right.

Another view of the underside of a male ornamental rainforest tarantula. Note the palpal bulbs.

LONGEVITY

There is a record of a tarantula collected at Mazatlan, Mexico which lived for an estimated 26-28 years. Longevities of 20 years or more are not uncommon for large N. American scrubland species such as the popular Mexican red-leg *(Euathlus smithi)* and California tarantulas *(Rhechosticta californica)*. As a general rule, large tarantulas from desert/scrubland habitats tend to be slow growing with a potential for long life while tropical tarantulas, particularly arboreal rainforest species tend to be fast growing and comparatively shorter lived. Much greater longevities will be obtained when working with captive-bred and raised-spiders, than with imports. As a rule, for any given species, the bigger the spider, the older it is likely to be.

What this means in practical terms is that many arboreal species can probably live 4 to 8 years in captivity unless they're males, in which case they may live less than two years. Large tropical forest species may live from three to ten years (possibly longer) while females of some of the large desert/scrubland species can be expected to exceed fifteen and possibly twenty years. As additional data becomes available, the potential longevities of various species in captivity will become clarified.

Trinidad chevron tree spider (*Psalmopoeus cambridgei*). A very attractive and popular arboreal species that should be kept warm and at a high relative humidity. Probable male (note more slender and spindly appearance) on left and probable female on right.

Male ornamental rainforest tarantula.

Tibial spur in male starburst baboon spider (*Pterinochilus murinus*).

Selecting Tarantulas

With the current variety now being offered, selecting a tarantula is not an easy process and careful consideration should be given to the matter. A key question will be what are your expectations from owning a tarantula. In general, people are interested in keeping live tarantulas for the following reasons

1. They want a different kind of pet that they can nonetheless handle.

" Hey Joey. Come on over and look at my spider. Let me pick it up and show it to you. Really its OK, he won't bite."

2. They want an impressive pet. Something which because of its size and unusual appearance will impress them and their friends.

" Can you believe the size of this king baboon spider?"
" Hey, you've just got to see that giant bird-eating spider that John has, it's supposed to be the biggest spider in the world. It's a mega spider, really rad!"

3. They want an interesting display with a different kind of animal.

"You've got to see this set up in Kathy's living room. It looks like a miniature jungle with all these little tree tarantulas in there. They're called pink-toed tarantulas. Little kids in Brazil are supposed to play with them and let them crawl all over them. It's kind of neat."

4. They have a scientific or hobbyist interest in them.

"Let me show you my collection of Poecilotherias. I've been recording growth rates, molting rates and maturity rates at different temperature and feeding schedules. I think the life span of these things can be altered by manipulating environmental factors."

Usually people's interests are combinations of one or more of the above. Taking into consideration one's expectations of keeping tarantulas, the following are some of the factors you should consider before selecting a tarantula.

- Some species tend to be tame and can be occasionally handled while others are fast and aggressive and can inflict a nasty bite.

- Many of the New World tarantulas will readily flick abdominal hairs when stressed. These hairs can cause strong allergic reactions in some people as well as itching worse than anything you may have ever experienced.

- Some species build dense webs which may make them problematical as display animals while most spin relatively small webs.
- Some species are so fast or so aggressive that maintenance can be problematical.

- There is a significant variation in the appearance of tarantulas. Many are plain brown colored, but some have neat contrasting patterns and others have attractive colors. Some tarantulas are heavy-bodied and massive in appearance with stout legs, while others will appear more spindly. Some have relatively long hairs on the abdomen and or legs, while others have a dense hair which will make them almost look as if covered in velvet.

Before selecting a tarantula, you should refer to the notes on species at the end of this book.

ADVANTAGES OF CAPTIVE-BORN TARANTULAS

Many of the captive-bred spiderlings currently imported from Europe and sold through specialized dealers are seldom more than 1/8 to 1/4 of an inch long and look like small ordinary house spiders. This is enough to make many a person nervous when one may have paid from ten to seventy-five dollars for a spiderling. Fortunately with a minimum of care, most spiderlings will thrive and grow rapidly into healthy, outstanding adults. If you want a healthy tarantula pet, nothing can beat a captive-bred animal. You will know its age, and you can have reasonable expectations of its life span. There is also a good chance that such animals will be relatively disease-free. If you are thinking about breeding, purchasing captive-bred spiderlings is a good way to synchronize breeding several years later. By purchasing a number of specimens, you have a reasonable chance of eventually having several sexually mature males and females. One should remember, however, that in many species including the popular red-leg tarantula, males will mature a year or more (sometimes two to three years) before females so purchasing and rearing spiders over several years may be required for eventually synchronizing reproduction.

ON BUYING TARANTULAS BY MAIL ORDER

It is the standard practice for dealers to state the size of various tarantulas species they have for sale. The current practice in the trade is to use leg-spread to indicate size.

SELECTING WILD-CAUGHT TARANTULAS

Most tarantulas sold in the general pet trade will be wild-collected adults. Careful observation and some common sense will improve your chances of selecting a tarantula that will fare well in captivity.

The following are general guidelines for selection:

1. The spider should appear alert and stand with its body held slightly above the ground. When prodded, it should demonstrate activity. A sluggish tarantula with its legs curled inward and body resting on the ground is ill. Tarantulas eventually die in this position with the legs curled in even more. Healthy tarantulas will demonstrate some type of reaction when they feel threatened. Alert New World species will frequently flick hairs from the abdomen. Others will raise their pedipalps and front legs. Many Old World species will rear up in an aggressive position. Many tarantulas will simply run away - the one exception to the above is if a spider is in the process of molting. During the pre molt period, tarantulas are typically sluggish. (but the legs still won't be curled in, actually the spider will probably be upside down with legs stretched out). In any case you don't want to buy a tarantula until it's done molting.

2. The abdomen should appear rounded though many wild-caught animals come in dehydrated and starved with depleted, shrunken abdomens. In many cases, these will plump up once the tarantulas are provided with a modicum of care. If the spider you are considering buying is expensive, let the dealer contend with the initial steps of establishing it to captivity. Many hobbyists will simply state that they are interested if the spider feeds (let the dealer introduce some crickets). Observe the spiders reactions. Don't spend a lot of money on an "iffy" spider. It will probably die.

3. If your mind is made up to purchase a tarantula, do a quick visual check of the animal for damage to the abdomen or other parts of the body. Avoid any spiders with a damaged abdomen or cephalothorax. Spiders with missing legs should not be of great concern because they will replace them over several molts. However, spiders with open wounds on legs are best avoided.

4. Unless you are interested in breeding, avoid males (see Sexing) which will be short-lived. Very large animals are probably relatively old and will not live as long as smaller animals.

BALD ABDOMENS AND MISSING LEGS

The primary defense of many New World tarantulas are urticating hairs located on the abdomen. When stressed or threatened, many species will flick hairs off the abdomen using their hind legs. Others release hairs upon contact or drop hairs while certain species are said to incorporate hairs in their webs. As a result, many species of New World tarantulas including the popular Mexican red-leg and giants such as the goliath bird-eating spider *(Theraphosa leblondi)* and *Pamphobeteus* species will commonly have bare patches on their abdomens. This is not a sign of old age as indicated in one popular book on tarantulas. These spiders will simply regenerate their hairy patches following their next molt.

Among imported tarantulas, there are occasionally individuals that arrive with a missing leg. As long as there is no bleeding and the dismembered area appears to be healed, these handicapped spiders will usually fare well and, in time, over several molts (unless they are males and have a limited number of molts available to maturity) completely regenerate the missing limb.

INITIAL ACCLIMATION OF IMPORTED TARANTULAS

Many imported animals are stressed because of inadequate relative humidity, inadequate temperature, dehydration, and starvation. The author recommends setting up the animal in a plastic jar type of set-up on a damp paper towel at the proper temperature and with a small shallow container of water. Before introducing the spider, mist the container lightly. The next day, offer food. If the animal is thin, offer one food item daily until the weight appears adequate.

The goliath bird-eater (*Theraphosa leblondi*) is the largest of the living spiders. These aggressive large spiders readily feed on larger prey such as immature mice and cockroaches. High relative humidity and warmth are essential for their successful maintenance. Note the partially bald abdomen. This species readily flicks off urticating hairs.

Housing and Maintenance

Serious arachnoculturists, particularly those keeping tree tarantulas and other fast moving species should keep them in a special room, which should be open spaced, and designed for efficient maintenance of a large collection. In addition, the room should be uncluttered and modified to be escape-proof so that any spider escaping in the course of maintenance is easily recovered.

APPROACHES TO KEEPING TARANTULAS

Depending on one's purposes there are two approaches to keeping tarantulas. One approach is a purely functional one which will prove useful to animal dealers, pet stores, hobbyists and researchers who want to keep large numbers of tarantulas under simple easily maintained conditions which allow for easy monitoring of the animals. With this approach, either jars or small plastic terraria are used to house single animals. Damp paper towels will be the preferred medium for maintenance. With larger enclosures for long term maintenance, hobbyists will sometimes use moist vermiculite which will have to be changed less frequently. The problem with vermiculite is that it makes transfer of animals into other containers more difficult (you can't simply transfer a tarantula from one jar to another) and cleaning/replacing will be more tedious.

The second approach to tarantula keeping attempts to simulate some of the essential features of a tarantula's natural habitat for the purpose of observing more natural behaviors, for breeding or simply to satisfy the decorative whims of the hobbyist.

NUMBER OF ANIMALS PER ENCLOSURE

Tarantulas of most species should be kept singly in a given enclosure or they will fight with the result that at least one of the animals will die. As a rule, small tarantulas are readily eaten by larger ones. There are exceptions to keeping one animal per enclosure. Arboreal species such as ornamental tarantulas (*Poecilotheria sp.*) and pink-toed tarantulas (*Avicularia*) will fare well in colony situations as long as the enclosures are large, the spiders are about the same size, and they are kept well fed. Other species may be suitable for colony keeping, but this will require experimentation and an occasional sacrifice.

ENCLOSURES

PLASTIC JARS

One of the author's favorite enclosures for keeping smaller tarantulas are the clear plastic jars now readily available in supermarkets or department stores. The advantage of these jars is that they allow for good visibility, they are lightweight, they are more or less unbreakable and easy to clean. The unbreakable aspect is a plus because it will prevent an escape or possibly death in case the jar should accidentally be dropped. The jars typically come in pint, half gallon and gallon sizes ideal for raising tarantulas from spiderling to subadult and finally adult size. The plastic lids can easily have a hole drilled in them or burned through using a small soldering iron (do this in an area with good ventilation i.e outdoors to avoid breathing the fumes). As a substratum one can use either paper towel or a layer of barely moistened vermiculite. Using paper toweling has the advantage of readily allowing the transfer of a spider from one jar to another by simply tilting one jar onto the mouth of another jar and gently tapping the spider in. The screw on lid will make the jar escape-proof.

The tall, one gallon jars will prove particularly suitable for arboreal species such as *Avicularia Psalmopoeus* or *Poecilotheria*. All one needs to do is add a single piece of cork bark as a vertical shelter.

GLASS STORAGE JARS
Same as above except that they're breakable, they're comparatively heavy and can chip in the course of procedures such as transferring a spider from one jar to another.

PLASTIC TERRARIA
Alternative containers for large spiders are the plastic "terraria" now sold in most pet stores. The one problem is that the top may provide too much ventilation to assure an adequate build-up of relative humidity within the enclosure. Sheet plastic can be placed on top or on the sides of the top to reduce evaporation of water from the container. These containers come in a variety of sizes suitable for maintaining most tarantulas except for tiny spiderlings which will readily escape through the ventilation holes of the lids. An advantage of these containers is that they provide more room than jars. They also come with secure tightly fitting lids. A disadvantage is that in time the sides tend to become scratched in the course of maintenance and the visibility diminished.

CLEAR PLASTIC AND TRANSLUCENT PLASTIC STORAGE BOXES
Plastic storage boxes are readily obtainable in drugstores and large department stores. The clear plastic shoe boxes and sweater boxes so popular for raising snakes are very suitable for housing tarantulas. They can be set on shelves with a heat cable placed in a routed groove on the top of the shelf that can be regulated with a rheostat. Semi-translucent plastic boxes will also work well. The tops of these boxes can easily (polystyrene) be perforated by using a soldering iron. These larger boxes are not suitable for rearing spiderlings, because there is enough of a space between the lid and the box that a spiderling could escape. There are, however, small rectangular clear plastic boxes with tight-fitting lids that will be suitable.

Plastic storage jars are ideal for the maintenance of large numbers of tarantulas. These allow for easy monitoring and display of various tarantulas and are therefore highly recommended for specialized stores and dealers.

A plastic terrarium commonly sold in the pet trade. With moistened vermiculite at the bottom, a section of cork and a shallow water dish (plastic floor guard), such setups are ideal for keeping most species of tarantulas including the popular Chilean rose tarantula (*Grammostola gala*). For rainforest species, the top will have to be partially covered to increase relative humidity. The main problem with plastic "terrariums" is that they are difficult to heat.

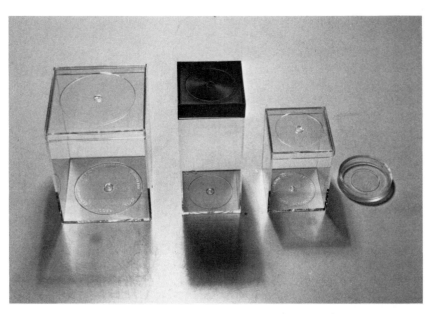

Various plastic storage boxes useful for raising and displaying tarantulas and a clear plastic floor guard (useful for offering water) sold in large department stores.

A setup for ornamental rainforest tarantulas (*Poecilotheria regalis*). The plant is a weeping fig (*Ficus benjamina*). A pair of ornamental rainforest tarantulas dwell in the center cork hollow. They will often emerge in the evening. Note the sliding side door to minimize the risk of escape during maintenance.

These may be difficult to find. Some of the import stores and stores specializing in plastics will usually carry them. These small boxes are also useful for transferring or capturing spiders.

ALL GLASS TANKS

All glass tanks sold in pet stores can be used for keeping tarantulas as long as one acquires a secure, tight-fitting lid. The sliding glass lids sold for covering fish tanks usually have openings for tubing or filter outlets that make them unsatisfactory for keeping tarantulas. The best thing to do is to buy a piece of plexiglas cut to size. Perforate it with a few holes and screw it onto a tight-fitting wood frame. All-glass tanks with sliding screen covers and sides are good choices for keeping tarantulas, because the covers can close in a manner that will prevent escape. The problem with screen covers is that they allow for a high evaporation rate. A thin piece of clear plastic or Plexiglas should be placed on top of the screen to reduce evaporation rate and increase relative humidity.

Tanks that also have a sliding screen front door are particularly well suited for maintaining and displaying arboreal species such as pink-toed tarantulas *(Avicularia)*, Indian and Sri Lankan tarantulas *(Poecilotheria)*, stout-legged baboon *(Heterscodra)* and feather-legged baboon *(Stromatopelma)*. The side door will allow or maintenance without disturbing the spiders and without the risk of them scurrying out the top (which they will tend to do).

CUSTOM-MADE ENCLOSURES

By using precut panels of glass or Plexiglas, custom-made enclosures can be built to suit your particular needs. Combinations of Plexiglas and glass can also work well. For example, use black Plexiglas for all sides except a glass front for better viewing (Plexiglas tends to scratch more easily and care is required when cleaning). Plexiglas cylinders are also available from specialized dealers.

COVERS

All tarantula enclosures should have secure covers, either screw on lids or hinged or sliding covers or tight-fitting wood frame and perforated Plexiglas covers. The cover of a tarantula enclosure will play a key role in regulating the evaporation rate within the enclosure and in maintaining an adequate relative humidity. Species from desert/scrubland type of habitats will fare well in enclosures with partially screened covers while tropical forest species will do best in covers that are 80-90% Plexiglas or glass with small air holes or screened areas to allow for some air exchange and ventilation.

GROUND MEDIA

Depending on one's purposes, the following media can be used as substrates for keeping tarantulas.

Paper towels

These are absorbent, they can readily be moistened and are easily replaced and disposed of. A good medium for animal dealers who may have to maintain large numbers of spiders yet have a quick turn over of stock. A good medium for initial quarantining of spiders. Feces will be readily observable on paper toweling. An ideal medium for hobbyists raising spiders in jars. One advantage when using paper towels is that quick spiders such as many of the arboreal tarantulas can be easily transferred from jar to jar without the mess of other media. One disadvantage of paper towel is that it needs to be changed regularly or it will mold. Other disadvantages are that paper towels will become slushy if too wet, and they will dry out relatively quickly if not regularly misted. Finally, paper toweling does not allow for burrowing. Nonetheless, this is the author's preferred medium for rearing species from spiderlings, particularly arboreal species. Using paper towel will force one to monitor and regularly maintain one's spider. It is easy to neglect or not notice spiderlings which can be invisible most of the time when maintained under more naturalistic conditions.

Vermiculite

This medium is highly recommended by tarantula keepers in Europe. It is aesthetically appealing, relatively sterile, retains moisture, is light, airy and allows for easy burrowing. It should be moistened prior to use by mixing with water until it is just damp (equal amounts of vermiculite and water by weight works well. An alternative is to mix one part water to 12-15 parts vermiculite by volume). After introduction, regular misting should help maintain an adequate moisture level. At least two grades of vermiculite are available. For small spiderlings, the fine grade is more recommended. For larger ones, the coarse grade. If a thick layer is used, burrowing spiders will readily construct burrows in it. Vermiculite is highly recommended for rearing spiderlings of burrowing species, such as king baboon spiders *(Citharischius crawshayi)*. **Generally, vermiculite is the best all purpose ground medium for keeping and displaying tarantulas.**

Gravel

Some hobbyists will use a fine gravel such as a smooth #3 aquarium gravel for keeping tarantulas from semi/arid areas. Gravel will often work well with larger spiders. It will retain some water between individual grains and pebbles. It can also be cleaned and changed when needed, but the weight is a problem (try carrying a large vivarium full of gravel). It usually doesn't allow for burrowing. Some people like the colored aquarium gravel for decorative purposes. Gravel is not suitable for keeping spiderlings.

Peat moss

For displaying tropical species requiring a high relative humidity, many hobbyists favor moist peat moss as ground medium. Peat moss does have the advantage of being able to absorb large amounts of water. One problem with peat moss is that any dead food items or discards tend to fungus. In time, various mites tend to colonize moist peat moss, unless one microwaves the peat moss before use. With burrowing spiders, this can be a touchy medium; it can be too moist at times or too dry which will cause the peat moss to cake. Some hobbyists will mix peat moss with potting soil. Avoid potting soil with perlite (it will tend to float to the surface). For keeping tropical arboreal species in enclosures with live plants, peat moss will work well as will peat moss mixed with potting soil.

Orchid bark

This type of bark consists of fir bark chips of various grades. If allowed to soak in water prior to introduction in the vivarium, orchid bark will absorb significant amounts of water. The best grade for keeping spiders is the fine or seedling grade. The positive features of this medium are the attractive appearance and ability to retain moisture without becoming soggy. The negative features are the coarse texture and weight which doesn't allow for burrowing. It is not suitable for keeping spiderlings which could accidentally get crushed between pieces of bark during maintenance. This medium can be used with good results with adults of arboreal and tropical forest species.

Sheet moss or sphagnum moss

These are available in both the reptile trade and the nursery trade. In some areas, sheet moss can be collected in the surrounding woods. Sheet moss works best when used for decorative purposes in combination with other media. Moistened sphagnum moss is often used as a medium for rearing tropical spiderlings because of its good moisture retaining qualities. The spaces between the loose strands will also provide a number of natural shelters which are readily used by spiderlings. Sphagnum moss is also a good medium for shipping tarantulas.

ARTIFICIAL BURROWS

There are ways of creating artificial burrows which will allow tarantulas that spend part of their time in burrows. This allows for more natural behaviors.

If you are interested in observing the behavior of tarantulas in burrows, one of the best methods of creating these burrows is to use floral foam sold through floral supply stores. The best are the 4 inch thick panels.

By using a saw, a section of foam can be cut to fit exactly within the vivarium. Prior to introducing the foam unit in the enclosure, you should carve out burrows at 45 degree angles from the surface, using a metal pipe of the desired diameter. You will find that for many spiders, it will be desirable to enlarge the width of the artificial burrow, so that it will actually have the shape of a flattened cylinder. At the bottom, an area can be carved out to create a subterranean cave of sorts. Burrows can also be created along the sides to allow for viewing once the foam unit is placed in the enclosure. The unit should be thoroughly washed under water to remove any loose foam particles. A layer of 2 inches of moist vermiculite should be placed at the bottom of the enclosure before introducing the unit. Once placed inside the tank, you will have created a situation where the relative humidity within the burrows will be significantly greater than at the surface, very much like the situation in the wild. For obvious reasons, one should regularly dampen the vermiculite.

Another method to encourage the formation of a burrow is to cut a section of rigid plastic tubing (for smaller animals) or PVC pipe and to bury it in the ground medium. Do not try to poke it through the medium, but dig out an area and place the pipe section at an angle with one opening at the soil surface. Poking pipe or tubing through a substrate medium results in clogged pipes that aren't particularly attractive to tarantulas.

SHELTERS

Most tarantulas will appreciate ground shelters. For arboreal species, vertical shelters should be provided (they will also serve as climbing areas). The best medium for creating tarantula shelters is cork bark. It looks natural, is light and is easily cleaned. For ground dwellers, other kinds of shelters can be used including the plastic shelters and painted concrete shelters sold in specialized reptile stores. For desert/scrubland species kept on a dry medium such as aquarium gravel or as a backup for tropical species, specially designed shelters can be used which include a shallow container with moist vermiculite to increase the relative humidity within the shelter. This will be beneficial for tarantulas that may be about to molt.

TEMPERATURE AND HEATING

Most tarantulas should be maintained at temperatures of 75-84 F. Some tropical species will fare well at the lower end of this range while others will fare better at the higher. As a rule, keeping tarantulas at 78-82 F will be satisfactory for most species. Semi-desert/scrubland species from temperate climates will tolerate cooler temperatures in the 60's during the winter. Tropical species from higher altitudes or montane forest will tolerate cooler night temperatures in the low 70's.

The general issue of heating tarantula enclosures is somewhat problematic. Individuals with a large collection will usually maintain their entire collection in a room heated with an electric heater regulated with a thermostat. It is wise to invest in a backup thermostat with such heaters. There are cases in which entire collections have been lost because of a faulty thermostat causing the heater to run continuously and cooking one's entire collection.

A humidified shelter. A container of moist vermiculite is placed inside a shelter to raise the relative humidity. This is recommended with all desert/scrubland tarantulas kept on a dry substrate. This is also recommended when keeping desert scorpions.

A section of floral foam with a hole through it was placed on top of moist vermiculite to encourage a male starburst baboon to dig a burrow. The male did just that. It was removed for the sake of the picture. In the same enclosure, a female has formed a burrow under a piece of bark. The animals are well fed and successful breeding has probably occurred.

SUBMERSIBLE HEATERS

If you are keeping your tarantula in a large glass tank, then one method used by some hobbyists is to place a small submersible heater in a glass jar filled with water. The top of the jar is sealed except for a small opening for the electrical cord. The temperature can be adjusted by changing the setting of the thermostat on the heater. Use a thermometer in the vivarium and adjust the thermostat as needed. Allow at least an hour between settings once the vivarium has been covered again. These adjustments should be made prior to introducing a tarantula.

HOT ROCKS

In a larger container that allows plenty of room for a spider to get away from a hot rock, it's possible to use a hot rock as a heater, but place a flat rock over it to diffuse the heat. The surface temperature of the hot rock should be no more than 85 F. In a semi-sealed container, a hot rock will somewhat raise the temperature in an enclosure.

HEATING PADS AND REPTILE HEATING PADS

A heating pad set on low or medium, depending on one's needs, will efficiently heat larger tarantula vivaria. These should only be used under glass aquarium-type tanks preferably with a recessed bottom. The vivarium should be lifted at least 1/4 inch above the heating pad so as not to crush the heating elements or thermostat. At a high temperature and if in direct contact with the heating pad, aquarium bottoms will sometimes crack because of heat expansion. The commercially sold subtank reptile heating pads will also work well for tarantula vivaria except that most don't have thermostats and there is a risk of them getting too hot.

HEATING CABLES

These are sold through nursery supply stores, hardware stores and some specialized reptile dealers. The nursery heating cables which are used to heat seedling flats, can be buried into the ground, and can be set on the bottom of tarantula vivaria that has a thick layer of substrate. Read directions carefully on how to lay out these heating units. The other type of heating cables are sold in hardware stores to wrap around plumbing to prevent freezing in the winter. These have been used for years by herpetoculturists to heat reptiles. Heating cables can be laid out around a custom-designed cabinet and plugged into a thermostat or, as many herpetoculturists do, plugged into a light dimmer type of rheostat to adjust the temperature. A popular use of heat cables among herpetoculturists is to place them in a specially routed groove in the upper surface of the shelves. A layer of aluminum sheeting is placed on top to diffuse the heat. The heating unit is then connected to a rheostat. Clear plastic sweater boxes are placed on these shelves. The units are designed so a section of heat cable lies under only one side of a box. A thermometer can be placed in a box and, with adjustments of the rheostat, the desirable temperature maintained.

THERMOMETERS

At least one minimum/maximum thermometer should be used if your collection is kept in a room. To obtain the temperatures of individual containers, you can use standard mercury thermometers or the stick on high range thermometers now sold in the aquarium and reptile trades.

The author's favorite thermometers are the electronic type with digital read-out obtainable through electronic supply stores. These usually come with an outdoor sensor which one can place inside any enclosure or on the surface of a heat source if desired to get a temperature reading. The thermometer itself can be located in the room and will provide a continuous reading of the room temperature until one moves the switch to the outdoor setting. This will then give you a temperature readout from the sensor. The more expensive digital thermometers will even give a you a 24 hour minimum/maximum reading at the push of a button.

RELATIVE HUMIDITY

Maintaining an adequate relative humidity within the tarantula enclosure is a key aspect to successful tarantula keeping. If the relative humidity is too low, some of the tropical forest species will not fare well and most tarantulas will have problems or difficulties molting. Tropical rainforest species will die in molt without appropriate relative humidity.

The generally accepted guidelines for tarantulas are to keep desert/scrubland species at a relative humidity of 55-75% and tropical forest/rainforest species at 75-90% relative humidity.

It is recommended that the serious hobbyist purchase a hygrometer (available through nursery supply stores and biological supply businesses) to monitor the relative humidity in a tarantula "room" and in individual tanks. The relative humidity in jars or containers that are mostly covered will, for obvious reasons, tend to be adequate as long as there is moisture in the substratum.

INCANDESCENT LIGHTING

As a rule incandescent bulbs should be avoided as a light source for tarantula vivaria unless one uses very low wattage bulbs. If incandescent bulbs are used, they should be placed over an area of the vivarium cover that is screened and not covered with glass or Plexiglas, or placed high enough over the vivarium that little heat reaches it. The problem with using incandescent bulbs, is that there is a risk of overheating and of increasing the evaporation rate in the vivarium at the risk of dehydrating a tarantula. Low wattage (15-25 W) bulbs particularly red incandescent bulbs can usually be used safely with tarantulas. The benefit of low wattage red bulbs is that tarantulas, like many other nocturnal animals, will not feel disturbed by this type of lighting and will readily emerge and perform various activities.

FLUORESCENT LIGHTING

A preferable alternative is a single fluorescent fixture and bulb. This type of lighting unit will generate relatively little heat and comparatively soft light. For tropical species, if you are growing live plants in the vivarium, full-spectrum fluorescent bulbs such as Vita-Lite R are recommended. Full-spectrum lighting also brings out more natural colors in both the plants and the animals.

NATURAL LIGHTING

Finally, diffused light from a window (not direct sunlight) will usually be adequate for keeping tarantulas. Make sure that no direct sunlight strikes your tarantula enclosures. This will cook and dehydrate your spiders in a surprisingly short period of time.

LANDSCAPING/ PLANTS

In large vivaria designed for keeping tarantulas, plants can be included to create a simulation of a natural habitat. As a rule, these "naturalistic" vivaria are designed to satisfy aesthetic or decorative whims of humans more than actually trying to reproduce a spider's habitat.

Naturalistic type of setups generally work better with tropical forest or rainforest species than species from semi-arid habitats. These vivaria usually are recommended only for larger animals and not for rearing spiderlings. You will lose control on the raising of spiderlings and lose your ability to monitor them in setups that look like little man-made jungles (now where is that little bugger hiding?).

Introducing plants in pots that are concealed either in the burrowing medium or by landscape features has definite advantages when keeping spiders. Keeping plants adequately watered when they are planted directly in the vivarium substrate usually results in a substrate that is too wet for tarantulas and may flood a tarantula's burrow. Keeping plants in pots will eliminate this problem. With arboreal species and terrestrial species that don't form burrows, the vivarium can be designed like a terrarium by first placing a 1 -1 1/2 inch layer of pebbles for drainage followed by a 1 1/2-2 inch layer of a moist, peat-based potting soil. The plants can be planted directly in the medium. On top, to prevent continuous contact of a spider with a damp substrate, a layer of fine orchid bark can be placed. Species with which this will work include *Theraphosa*, *Lasiodora* and some of the *Pamphobeteus*. It will also work with all arboreal species. The following are some plants that will work in tarantula vivaria:

Pothos *(Scindapsus aureus).* One of the hardiest of vivarium plants.

Creeping fig *(Ficus pumila)*. A small leaved, fast growing vine.
Gold dust Dracaena *(Dracaena godseffiana)*
Leather leaf Dracaena *(Dracaena hookeriana)*
Dwarf umbrella plant *(Brassia actinophylla)*
***Calathea* species**
Snakeplants *(Sansevieria species)*. There are many varieties including forms with vertical leaves such as the popular *Sansevieria trifasciata* and others with relatively short rosettes, such as the birds-nest Sansevieria *(Sansevieria t. hahni)*.

Many other plants including certain ferns and even orchids such as the jewel orchid *(Haemaria discolor)* will work depending on the temperature, lighting and ventilation of your set-ups.

With species other than tropical species, it is best to use plants in pots concealed in the medium or by landscape features. There are currently some interesting vivarium shelters and decorations that incorporate artificial desert plants that are reasonably well designed and safe for use with species from semi-arid areas. Using live desert or succulent plants with desert scrubland tarantulas is not recommended, because the light required to grow these plants adequately will often generate too much heat or light to maintain desert tarantulas successfully within the environmental constraints of most vivaria.

Potted plants that can work with such species include small ponytail palms *(Beaucarnea recurvata)* which are quite adaptable, *Haworthia* species (African short succulents that for the most part form small rosettes of attractively patterned leaves such as *H. fasciata)*, *Gasteria* species, and dwarf aloes. Many other plants could be used with stronger lighting, heat and lower relative humidity at the surface of the vivarium but this would mean designing burrows with cooler temperatures and higher humidity and would require some ingenuity. There is a lot of room for innovative designs and experimentation in the area of naturalistic vivarium design for keeping tarantulas.

ARTIFICIAL PLANTS
Some of the life-like artificial plants can be used to decorate tarantula vivaria. For obvious reasons, plastic plants will be more easy to clean than silk plants, but some of the plastic coated silk plants tend to hold up rather well.

OTHER LANDSCAPE ITEMS
Freshwater driftwood, dried sections of palm trees, and interesting dried wood stumps can be used to enhance the appearance of a tarantula vivarium. Just remember to be careful when moving any landscape materials once installed in the vivarium. There is always the risk of accidentally crushing or injuring your spider. Natural cork bark because of its light weight is one of the best landscape items one can use.

An artificial burrow made of floral foam in a setup with a king baboon spider (*Citharischius crawshayi*). Damp vermiculite was placed at the bottom. Note the carved out cave to allow viewing from the side. These types of setups work well with many burrowing species.

The author's pink-toed tarantula setup. Five pink-toed tarantulas (*Avicularia avicularia*) live together in this twenty gallon vivarium. At the bottom is a layer of moist peat moss over which a thin layer of orchid bark was placed. The cover is 90% covered with plastic. A sliding side door prevents risks of escape. The plants are select plastic-coated silk-plants.

Maintenance

When rearing animals in jars and small containers, it is a good idea to establish a once to twice a week maintenance routine. which should include: Remove and replace parts of the medium that are dirty and remove any dead insect prey or other detritus, feed and replace water as needed and misting. As the animals become larger and their enclosures become more spacious, a once a week routine will usually be adequate.

BEWARE OF ANTS

Make sure that the areas you keep tarantulas in are free of ants and make sure you remove within a short period of time any dead uneaten insects or excess wastes. Dead crickets will readily attract ants. If you don't want to walk onto the horror of, say, your prize ornamental tarantulas that you've raised from babies, dead and consumed by a swarm of ants, you will heed this message. Large tarantulas appear somewhat more immune to ant attacks but it certainly can happen as many hobbyists can vouch. So watch out for the damned ants!

Keep insecticides ....far away.
Do not use insecticides near your tarantulas. If ants are a problem in a given area, remove the tarantulas from the area before treating with a spray. Ant traps are usually safe to use in surrounding areas. Think spider.

TOOLS

As a general rule, tarantulas are animals that should not be handled with the possible exception of a handful of species known to be generally docile. As a result, most arachnoculturists will use a number of tools to move and transfer tarantulas, and to facilitate maintenance routines.

The following are tools which will prove invaluable in the captive management of these animals:

LONG FORCEPS

Long forceps (10-12 in. tissue forceps) are one of the most important tools of the tarantula keeper. They can be used as a tool for safely pushing a tarantula out of the way or gently prodding it toward one side of an enclosure. They are ideal for removing uneaten or dead insects from enclosures. In planted enclosures, they will allow one to remove plant debris. They are great for picking out paper towel from jars or for lifting a shelter which might conceal a nasty spider.

PLASTIC FISH NETS

The plastic fish nets sold in pet stores are ideal for catching that swift tarantula that got out of the container while you were cleaning or transferring the animal. Some species of tarantulas such as the Indian rainforest tarantulas *(Poecilotheria sp.)* Asian tarantulas *(Haplopelma)* and Sunburst baboons *(Pterinochilus murinus)* are fast and can easily be lost without the proper tools. A fish net will prove to be the most effective tool for capturing these tarantulas. Different sizes can be used for different size animals and different purposes. Once the tarantula is immobilized under a fishnet, you can slip a piece of cardboard underneath and press it against the frame while you carry the spider back to its enclosure.

Caution: One should use common sense when capturing a tarantula with a fish net.. Do not slam the net down in a panic. Keep cool and be gentle. That hard plastic coated frame slapped down on your prized spiders could sure make a mess.

SQUARE CLEAR PLASTIC BOXES

A container with a crisp flat edge such as a clear plastic storage box (sold in a variety of stores) is perfect for catching escapee spiders because the edges will be flush with the ground. There are a variety of sizes available. The standard technique for catching spiders is to put the edge of a tilted box in front of a spider and from behind gently prod it into the box. Put the lid on or cover the top with a piece of cardboard as you carry the spider back to its enclosure.

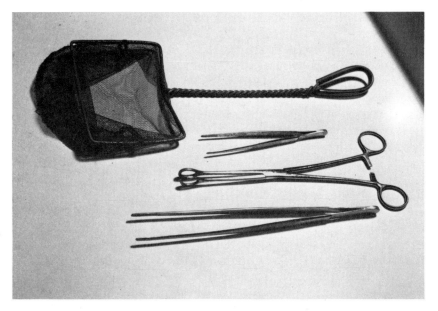

Tools for the arachnoculturist, a fish net, forceps and tongs.

Feeding

Tarantulas feed primarily on live insects of the appropriate size. Larger species may occasionally feed on small vertebrates. The following are recommended feeding regimens for tarantulas:

SPIDERLINGS

Captive-bred spiderlings will initially fare well on a diet of pinhead crickets (1-3 days old) or wingless fruit flies. Wingless fruit fly cultures can be bought from biological supply companies or through mail order live food suppliers that advertise in tropical fish magazines. Pinhead crickets can be special ordered through pet stores or can be easily hatched from adult crickets purchased at a pet store. Buy a couple of dozen crickets *(Acheta domestica)* and keep them in a plastic terrarium on a 1 1/2 inch layer of vermiculite. Provide a shelter made up of cardboard egg crate or sections of cork. Offer a slice of orange as a source of water and feed either tropical fish flakes or chicken mash or flaked cereal. The crickets will breed and lay hundreds of eggs in the damp (1 part water to 12-15 parts by volume) vermiculite. At 85 F eggs will hatch in 2-3 weeks. Another alternative food useful for the initial feeding of some spiderlings are tiny mealworms (see below).

SUBADULTS AND ADULTS

As the spiders grow, correspondingly larger insects can be offered. Commercially raised crickets are the all around best staple diet for rearing and maintaining tarantulas. It is recommended that crickets purchased in stores be kept for at least a day in a terrarium and offered orange and a nutritious food as mentioned in the previous section on raising spiderlings. In addition to crickets, commercially-raised mealworms including king mealworms *(Zoophobas)* can be offered as part of a tarantula diet. Medium to large mealworms are now readily available from many pet stores. These can be offered to larger tarantulas. Various tarantula species will vary in their tastes for mealworms, and one will have to experiment to determine whether an individual animal likes them or not. As a rule, tarantulas from desert/scrubland areas will be more apt to take mealworms then some of the tropical species, but this will vary from individual to individual. For example, the author has some pink-toed tarantulas *(Avicularia)* that would readily descend from their vertical shelter and grab a mealworm, while others would not.

Mealworms can also be cultured. The main advantage with this is that if you are involved in breeding tarantulas, you will find that tiny mealworms, which will have to be meticulously picked out from a culture can prove valuable as a food source for initial feedings of spiderlings of certain species such as orange-kneed tarantulas *(Euathlus emilia)* and *(Euathlus smithi)*. As a rule, mealworms should only make up a portion of a tarantula's diet until further experimentation clarifies whether they are nutritionally adequate for raising these spiders. Experimentation has shown that the nutritional value of mealworms can be boosted by placing them in a container with a nutritive vitamin supplemented diet such as chicken mash or flaked cereal with a high quality powdered bird or reptile mineral/multivitamin supplement. Most of the extra nutritional value comes from gut contents of the worms so initially depriving mealworms of food for 2-3 days before introducing them into the mix is recommended. Feed the worms within 12-24 hours of introduction in the mix.

With larger spiders, one to three day old "pink" mice can occasionally be offered. Very large spiders may even capture and feed on early stage "fuzzy" mice, but these rodent diets are by no means required, and tarantulas will fare well on a diet consisting exclusively of commercially raised insects.

PREY-SIZE CRITERIA

This aspect of tarantula feeding is something for which you get a feel after some experience. As a general rule, insect prey fed to tarantulas should be 1\4-1\3 the length of the spider body. What may be surprising to some is that even big spiders will readily take large numbers of relatively small prey when no larger prey is available, and large spiders will feed on insects 1/8 and even 1/16 of their body length. At the other extreme, feeding tarantulas prey that is too large may frighten them or can create problems following capture as the prey continues to struggle for long periods of time.

SCHEDULE OF FEEDING

Feeding regimens of tarantulas can vary depending on what species you are keeping and the amount of time you wish to devote to the maintenance of your spiders. If you are rearing spiderlings for the purpose of captive breeding, your goal will be for the animals to attain sexual maturity as quickly as possible and, therefore, to plan feeding regimens which will lead to optimal growth rates in the shortest periods of time. Depending on species, this may mean offering food every one to three days. In these cases, the regimens will depend on the temperature at which maintained and the species one is working with. Spiderlings of *Euathlus smithi* or *E. emilia* will not feed nor grow nearly as quickly as spiderlings of *Theraphosa leblondi* or *Lasiodora* species which may feed every one to two days during the growth periods of their lives. As a result of their voracious habits and rapid growth, *Lasiodora* and *Theraphosa* spiderlings may achieve leg spans of 4-5 inches in their first year. As spiders grow, their diets will be adjusted as one notices that they are no longer feeding as frequently as they used to.

As a general principle, tarantulas should be offered food twice a week particularly younger animals. Large animals (where adult size is reached and growth is minimal) of many species will fare well on feedings spaced every 7-10 days. Such extended feeding regimens should only be used with healthy animals with good weight. They should be modified if significant weight loss becomes apparent. More frequent feeding is recommended when conditioning the animals for breeding. If used with small spiderlings or small spiders an extended feeding regimen may stunt captive-raised animals and delay breeding (if that is ones' interest). Imported tarantulas with shrunken abdomens should be offered food every 1-2 days until they appear to have regained adequate weight.

HOW MUCH PER FEEDING

The number of prey items one introduces in a tarantula's enclosure will depend on the size of the prey items and the size of the tarantula. As a general rule, it is not a good idea to introduce more than two or three prey items at a time. If the prey items are relatively large, introduce only one at a time. This is particularly important when one is keeping tarantulas in small enclosures. A tarantula, which might readily feed on a single cricket introduced in a jar may feel threatened if one introduces five or six crickets at one time and refuse to feed. If the prey items are not too large, a tarantula will seize one prey item and if hungry will seize a second etc. Spiderlings will usually feed on single prey items, but large tarantulas may grab and have hold of two or three prey items at one time. Once a tarantula is done feeding, any uneaten prey items should be removed with forceps.

When not hungry, tarantulas can be stressed by the action of large crickets moving about their enclosure and running into them. If tarantulas are molting, loose insects can be stressful and possibly harmful. With smaller spiders, there is also a risk that they could become victims of starved crickets left in their enclosures unless one provides food for the crickets

MY TARANTULAS WILL NOT FEED

Tarantulas will fast for varying periods of time in the course of their lives:
- All tarantulas stop feeding for at least a day and sometimes several days prior to and following molting.
- Tarantulas will not feed if they are kept too cool.
- Tarantulas will refuse food if they have had a problematic molt.
- Tarantulas will refuse food if they are sick.
- Tarantulas will refuse food if they are already so stuffed that they can't eat any more.
- Sometimes tarantula fast for reasons for which we don't necessarily have an explanation.
- Don't worry if your tarantula is off feed. If it is healthy, it could live for weeks or months (the latter is mostly true for species from semi-arid areas) without feeding.

WATER

The author has raised many tarantulas without ever offering water in a dish, but rather by misting the enclosure lightly every two to three days. In these containers, humidity is maintained at 70% or more, and the evaporation rate is relatively low. A hand sprayer should be a primary source of water for smaller spiders. and the adjustment on the nozzle tightened so that only a fine mist is generated. With imported adult spiders and with larger captive-raised spiders, a small, shallow container of water should be placed in the tank. Suitable water containers include plastic bottle caps and the clear plastic floor guards sold in hardware stores to place under the legs of furniture. When fed insect prey that has been properly maintained prior to feeding, tarantulas probably also obtain a significant amount of water from ingested prey, i.e., the orange that crickets have stored in their guts.

A setup for keeping large numbers of tarantulas. Translucent plastic storage boxes are maintained on shelves. At the bottom of each shelf,. a heat cable in a routed groove provides heat which is adjusted with a rheostat. Photo by Russ Gurley.

Molting

Molting or shedding the of old exoskeleton is a critical period for tarantulas. As a spider nears molting, it becomes more sluggish and stops feeding. About twenty-four hours prior to molting a tarantula may be so sluggish, that it may appear dead. Many tarantulas flip on their backs prior to molting, others molt while lying on their sides. When you notice these odd behaviors, control your first impulse, which may be to poke or flip over your tarantula to make sure it is ok. If it isn't, no amount of poking will resuscitate it. If it's molting you may cause fatal injuries to your spider. Spiderlings initially molt frequently, every few weeks or so. As they become older, they molt less frequently. Adults may only molt once a year. During molting, the old exoskeleton splits and forms a shell from which the spider must extricate itself. Under the old exoskeleton the spider which has a new and relatively soft exoskeleton must struggle to get out. During that time, the soft skinned spider can easily be injured. If conditions aren't right a spider may split its new soft exoskeleton and bleed to death. A critical factor for successful molting is high relative humidity, at least 55% for most tarantulas and 70% or more for tropical forest species. Many first time tarantula keepers lose their spiders during molting, because they keep them under the dry conditions erroneously recommended by many pet stores at the time of writing (plastic terrarium, dry gravel, and a small shelter are the basic recommendations of many pet stores, little emphasis is placed on relative humidity). If tarantulas are kept under the conditions recommended in this book, there should be no problems with molting. Sometimes, tarantulas have problematic molts which result in some bleeding and possibly incomplete molting of the skin. These tarantulas may go off feed for months or bleed to death and die within a few days following a molt. Follow the care instructions in this book, and this will not happen. A light misting once or twice a day is beneficial when a tarantula is suspected to be molting. Following a molt, withhold food for a couple of days to allow the exoskeleton to harden. Tarantulas will resume feeding after a day or more depending partially on size.

A Chilean rose tarantula (*Grammostola spatulata*) which has just molted. The high relative humidity which can be maintained in these jars (only a small hole is drilled in the lid) minimizes the risk of molting problems. Under drier conditions, Chilean rose and other tarantulas may have problematic molts that can prove fatal.

An assortment of molted exoskeletons from different species.

Handling

Some books will tell you that the safe way to pick up a tarantula is to grab them by the cephalothorax between a thumb and index finger positioned between the second and third pair of legs. That's all fine and dandy, but the fact is that this method works best with species which have a propensity to be docile such as Mexican red-legs or Chilean rose tarantulas; species which most people will either let crawl on their hands or transfer and move by other methods. Try this cephalothorax grabbing technique on a baboon spider or an Asian bird-eating spider, and you may be wondering how come it didn't work and you now have two painful puncture marks at the end of a finger. Furthermore, the people who really want to handle tarantulas don't want to just grab one and lift it in the air, they want to feel the thing crawl on them. They want to cross the contact gap between spiders and men. Some think it feels neat. Others want to establish more of a rapport with their spider.... It is interesting that popular books that tell you how you shouldn't handle your tarantula invariably have several explicit photos of people doing just what you're not supposed to do. The fact is that many people who buy tarantulas want a tarantula pet.

TARANTULA PETS

Only a few tarantulas are suitable for handling, primarily New World species which were once grouped under the subfamily *Grammostolinae* (now in the Theraphosinae). Species available in the pet trade include N. American species such as the Mexican red-leg and orange-kneed tarantulas, some of the Central American *Euathlus*, and a small number of South American species such as the Chilean rose. In addition, pink-toed tarantulas currently being imported from Guyana also tend to be reluctant biters, but have the disadvantage of being fast moving. With many other species, such as the large South American *Theraphosa* and *Lasiodora* and particularly with Old World tarantulas such as baboon spiders or the Asian bird-eating spiders of the pet trade, you risk a bite. Finally there are tarantulas which, though they may be reluctant to bite, are so fast that handling them is definitely not recommended. If you need to have a tarantula that you can handle, stick to the tried and true species such as Mexican red-legs, Chilean rose, Chilean flame (not as calm as the rose) and pink-toed tarantulas (fast and difficult but don't usally bite).

One of the biggest risks when handling tarantulas is that they may accidentally fall from a certain height and split their abdomens upon impact. Tarantulas with split abdomens usually die though some luck has been had applying a quick drying glue to hold the split edges together and one may consider experimenting with the use of Crazy Glue R for this purpose. Of course, what one should do is practice safe handling procedures that will prevent this from ever happening in the first place. If you must handle your tarantula, do it while sitting at a table, preferably in an area which has a carpet floor. Another good place to handle tarantulas is while sitting on a sofa or on a stuffed armchair in a room with carpet flooring. An unpleasant side effect of handling New World tarantulas is that many species flick off urticating hairs when stressed or simply drop them in the course of handling. These urticating hairs can itch like hell and cause severe allergic reactions in some people. Getting tarantula hairs in your eyes or mouth is definitely no fun so don't let them climb on your face.

BITES

Tarantulas, because of their large size, have been the cause of a considerable amount of myth and superstition relating to the deadliness of their bites. Popular myths perpetuated by various jungle movies (including Tarzan whom you would assume should know better), spy movies (i.e., James Bond 007) and science-fiction type horror movies such as the popular movie Arachnophobia (it provided thrills even to those of us who know better) and the sci-fi horror classic "Tarantula" suggest that big and horrible means deadly. These movies play on our worst fears about spiders when we were children. If little spiders are scary because they can jump on you and scurry in the damnedest spaces to bite you, giant spiders are creatures that have crawled out of your worst nightmares. The actual issue of tarantula bites and the effects of their venoms is not very clear and requires further investigation.

There have been some studies for example with members of the South American genus *Acanthoscurria* to determine the effects of their bites on mice (they die in 20-30 minutes), but speculating from the effects of spider bites (or scorpion bites for that matter) on laboratory animals to make generalization on the effects of their bites on humans may not always be reliable. By the same token, generalizing from the studies that have been made on the effects of certain N. American tarantulas (as have some authors of tarantula books) to conclude with broad statements that tarantulas are relatively harmless is also probably wrong.

Using anecdotes gathered during field studies as a source of information on bites, invariably ends up being of little value because the reports of "facts" are distorted or superseded by popular superstition. For example, in parts of Africa, rapid death or delayed death (up to a year after the bite) is a common theme of these superstitions relating to bites by tarantulas. In addition there can also be confusion as to the source of a reported bite. A bite by another type of spider such as a trapdoor spider or black widow (Latrodectus species) can quickly get blamed on the larger, scarier and sometimes hissing (stridulating) tarantula.

Finally, the biggest drawback to acquiring reliable information on the effects of tarantula bites is that there are not that many reports of humans actually bitten by tarantulas. As a result, we can only speculate from the relatively limited amount of available information.

We know or at least strongly suspect from the available data that many tarantulas probably have a bite whose consequence is seldom more than that of a bee sting. The author has also been unable to find a single substantiated report of a human being dying as a result of a tarantula bite. But the above generalizations, because of a relative lack of actual reports may be misleading. In many cases we have a situation where we won't really know what happens until it happens.

As more exotic species are becoming available in the trade, it is important to deal with all these species in a responsible manner that precludes putting one in a position of being bitten. Humans react differently to animal venoms, and caution is warranted until more information becomes available in this area. Certainly, children should never be allowed to handle or keep anything but the most gentle and better known New World species (and even then only with parental supervision). Tarantulas are primarily interesting display animals and there is no need to expose oneself to the possibility of a bite by attempting to handle or "tame" a given species. If you inspect a tarantula's fangs, it should occur to you that even being punctured by two relatively large fangs should not be a particularly pleasant experience. If you've ever felt a large tarantula attempt to bite a pair of stainless steel forceps, fangs scraping against the metal, you know what I'm talking about.

Though no tarantula to date can be considered deadly, several species can inflict bites which will result in local effects of varying severity including reddening of the affected area, pain, swelling, joint pains and cramps. Fortunately, these symptoms often disappear after periods ranging from a few hours to a few days. Some of the species known to cause such symptoms include Asian ornamental tarantulas *(Poecilotheria species)* and the sunburst baboon *(Pterinochilus murinus)*. Individuals bitten by red-leg tarantulas have reported pain and swelling. The author has been told of a bite by a *Theraphosa* with painful local effects (including swelling of the affected limb) severe enough that the victim was not about to repeat the experience. Caution is also generally recommended with tarantulas of the genera *Lasiodora* and *Pamphobeteus*.

At least one tarantula *Harpactirella lightfooti* (a baboon spider), has apparently produced systemic effects following a bite. The report described pain at the site of the bite, periods of continuous vomiting, shock, and collapse. Many dealers in the U.S. suggest caution when dealing with some of the Asian and Indonesian Selenocosmid spiders which are now becoming available on the U.S. market.

So what is one to conclude from this? To date, it appears that as a whole, tarantulas are not particularly dangerous and not of significant medical importance. It is, however, possible that several species for which there is little data on bites may turn out to be more dangerous than initially believed. For this reason, the author advocates caution when dealing with most of the species currently available on the market. Why put yourself in a position of being a human guinea pig? Because of the growing interest in this group of spiders, one can expect future studies in this area which, hopefully, will clarify this topic. So be smart and deal with your animals in a responsible manner.

STRIDULATION

Many Old World tarantulas and some New World tarantulas have the ability to stridulate, essentially producing a sound resembling a hiss by rubbing body structures (chelicerae, palps and or parts of the first legs) together. This is used as an effective defensive behavior. Anyone who has seen a king baboon spider rear up in a defensive position and stridulate knows that the hiss-like sound can be a significant deterrent. The structure of stridulating organs are useful taxonomic tools in identifying subfamilies, genera and species.

Female starburst baboon spider (*Pterinochilus murinus*). This is a popular small species which is easily bred. It is fast moving and best displayed in a setup where it can form burrows.

Breeding

With the increased interest in tarantulas and the high prices of certain collector's species, we can expect the development of large scale captive-breeding of tarantulas in the United States. It is beyond the scope or intent of this book to elaborate on the captive breeding of various tarantula species.

A generalized model for the captive breeding of tarantulas appears to be as follows:

1. One must have adult animals of both sexes. In females, size can be a criterion for maturity, but it must be remembered that females often take longer than males to mature. If raising a group of spiderlings for breeding, it is wise to obtain spiderlings over a two or three year period to synchronize breedings. Mature males can be sexed by their swollen palpal bulbs (ends of the pedipalps) and the associated spine-like intromittent structures called emboli. In addition, males of many species acquire characteristic tibial hooks or spurs once they have reached maturity.

2. A few weeks following its adult molt, a male will construct a special type of web called a sperm web on which it will produce an ejaculate containing spermatozoa. The male then absorbs the ejaculate into its palpal bulbs. Following this process, a male will tend to become unusually active, and this will be the right time to introduce a male into a female's enclosure. If all is right the male will proceed relatively rapidly to mate with the female by eventually introducing the palpal bulbs into the female's epigynum. The sperm is then stored in the females spermathecae to be eventually used for fertilization of ova. In some species, such as the Sunburst baboon *(Pterinochilus murinus)*, there appears to be evidence of stored sperm being used to fertilize more than one set of eggs.

With arboreal species kept in a community set-up, males and females are kept together at all times and breeding will happen when they are ready. With most other species, males should be removed following successful breeding of a female.

3. Depending on the species, several weeks or several months following mating, a female will produce an egg-case. In several North American species, such as the Texas brown tarantula *(Rhechosticta hentzi)* and the Mexican red-leg (Euathlus *smithi)*, mating in the fall of one year will result in the female laying eggs the following late spring or summer. The female normally guards the egg sac and may change its position presumably to provide adequate conditions for egg development. The eggs hatch in two weeks to three months. Some breeders will remove the egg case and place it in an incubator with proper heat and relative humidity. Developing eggs may be attacked by fungi if kept too wet or desiccate if kept too dry. A few dead eggs will also attract certain small species of flies which will feed on the eggs. It has been recommended that egg sacs be turned at least once a day but several arachnoculturists have had success with no or infrequent turning depending on the species and the conditions under which the egg sacs were maintained.

4. Spiderlings can initially remain with the mother, but should eventually be removed and placed in a container with damp sphagnum. At first, most breeders keep spiderlings in groups, but eventually spread them out into individual containers. If kept in groups, cannibalism is likely to occur.

Ants will readily swarm and kill tarantulas, particularly spiderlings. Keeping individual rearing jars in a low level of water will eliminate this problem. These are captive-bred orange-knee tarantulas (*Euathlus emilia*). The lids of the jars were removed for the photograph.

Raising Captive-bred Tarantulas

The author has successfully raised several species of tarantulas from spiderlings with minimal mortality. The following procedures are recommended.

Purchase pint-sized plastic jars or similar containers. Punch or drill one or two tiny (small enough that a spiderling couldn't go through) holes in the lid for air exchange. Place a layer of paper towel at the bottom of the jar. In one corner, place a small piece of moist sheet moss. Using a hand sprayer adjusted for very fine misting, lightly mist the inside.

Introduce the spiderling. Offer crickets half the length or less than the spiderlings. For just hatched spiderlings, offer pinhead crickets or wingless fruit flies; offer larger prey animals as they grow older. Don't offer more than a spiderling will feed on. Feed every three days. Remove uneaten crickets within three hours of introduction.

Adjust cricket size as the spiders grow larger. Mist lightly two to three times a week. Do not allow paper towel to become completely dry. Never allow the paper towel to become soaked. It should be just damp. Initially, change paper towel and clean jar every week to ten days, then more frequently as the animal becomes larger. To clean, have an extra jar ready and transfer the spiderling to an alternate jar between cleanings.

When dealing with large numbers of spiderlings, some hobbyists have successfully used small clear plastic storage boxes with moistened sheet moss on the bottom. An advantage to this is that it allows one to keep a lot of spiderlings in a minimal amount of space. When using just sheet moss, one can wait several weeks before having to clean the box and replace the medium.

KEEPING RECORDS ON SPECIES

Much valuable information can be obtained from keeping records on the species that one is keeping. If one is raising spiders from spiderlings for the purpose of breeding, recording the number of molts to maturity will provide invaluable information on the life history of these animals. When combined with methodical controls on temperature and feeding regimens, recording growth (body length, leg span and weight) as well as molting rates will provide information on how environmental conditions may affect the rate of growth or maturity. Recording behaviors including web design and feeding will also prove worthwhile. Relatively little is known of the behavior of tarantulas, and there are unlimited

Theraphosa leblondi Obtained: 7/21/91
Source: Import, Guyana. Purchased at Reptile Haven
Body length: 72 mm. Note: Probably ♀

Date		date		date			Notes
7/23/91	1 fuzzy mouse	8/18/91	refuse	9/4/91	refuse web		8/15/91 - Room overheated, container dry - sprayed with water -
7/27/91	1 fuzz mouse	8/21/91	refuse	9/9/91	refuse		
7/29/91	1 roach	8/24/91	refuse	9/23/91	egg case		9/14/91 Built large flat web -
8/3/91	1 fuzz mouse	8/29/91	1 roach				
8/7/91	4 crickets	8/30/91	refuse				9/23/91 egg case -
8/12/91	1 roach	9/4/91	refuse				
8/15/91	refuse	9/9/91	1 fuzz mouse				

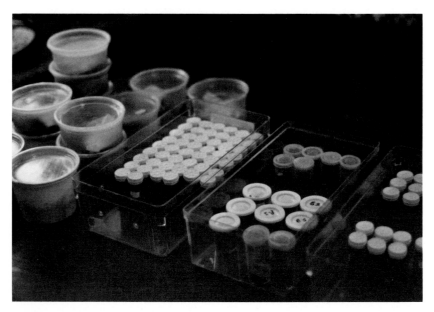

A setup for maintaining and raising large numbers of individual spiderlings. Photo by Russ Gurley.

Asian black velvet tarantula *(Haplopelma minax)*. These fast and secretive spiders can be aggressive.

Chilean flame tarantula *(Grammostola spatulata)*. An attractive docile and popular species with strong orange highlights.

Notes on Popular Species

Mexican red-leg *(Euathlus smithi)*

At the time of writing, this species which is listed under CITES Appendix II (threatened and requiring special permits for transport or transfer between countries) can not be legally exported out of Mexico without the appropriate paperwork. Most available animals (and they are few and far between) are captive-bred and/or raised spiderlings or old pets purchased before the species was protected. Mexican red-legs are, however, regularly offered as captive-bred spiderlings out of Europe.

The Mexican red-leg tarantula remains one of the most beautiful and desirable of the tarantulas and is characterized by its heavy bodied proportions, attractive rich colors including the orange-red on the legs, a relatively good disposition, hardiness and a potential for long life. What more can one ask for? This is one of the best. The main complaint about this species is its readiness to flick abdominal hairs when stressed. This shouldn't be much of a problem if you don't handle your spider. If you do, be forewarned that some people develop severe allergic reactions to the hairs.

Mexico should consider developing this species as an economic resource. By harvesting the egg sacs of females and rearing the young under captive conditions, large numbers could be raised, a small percentage could be released to the wild; a substantial and valuable crop could be developed.

In England, captive-breeding of this highly desirable species is done with some regularity. Unlike tropical forest tarantulas which will grow at an amazingly fast rate, desert species such as the red-leg tend to grow considerably slower. Males reach sexual maturity at about the twentieth instar (stage between molts) at an age of 4-5 years. Females will mature two to three years later than males, a factor which would prevent inbreeding in the wild. Females lay several hundred eggs. In captivity, raised under optimal conditions these spiders may reach sexual maturity at a younger age than their wild counterparts. Keep as a desert/scrubland species. This species can live twenty years or more with several records of specimens over twenty-four years old.

Orange-knee tarantula or painted tarantula *(Euathlus emilia)*

Except for coloration, whatever has been said about *E. smithi* pretty much applies here. As a pet not quite as calm as *E. smithi*. This species is regularly available as captive-bred spiderlings out of Europe and not regulated by CITES. Like all Mexican animals, it cannot be legally exported out of Mexico at this time.

Striped-knee or zebra tarantula *(Rhechosticta seemanni)*

At the time of writing, this attractive species is being imported from Nicaragua. This is a medium-sized tarantula which is variable in color, individuals varying between a rich brown and a gray black. In some individuals, the chelicerae and other anterior parts of the body can be a beautiful powder gray-blue when viewed in sunlight. The distinctive features of this species are the fine white markings running the length of the legs. It should be maintained like tropical forest tarantulas at a temperature of 78-84F and relative humidity of 80% or more. The author is currently keeping this species in a setup with artificial burrows. In this type of display, this species is one of the more interesting species to observe. Striped-knee tarantulas will emerge from their burrows when hungry but eventually rush back into the burrow at the least disturbance. Many spend large amounts of time "sitting" at the entrance of their burrows. One of the most beautiful of the tarantulas and one of the author's favorites.

Chilean rose-haired tarantula *(Grammostola gala)*

At the time of writing, this is one of the most readily available tarantulas in the U.S. pet trade. This moderately large species has a subtle beauty as suggested by its popular name. One of its most desirable features is its relative docility. This is one of the most recommended tarantulas for those wishing a gentle handleable spider. Doesn't readily flick abdominal hairs, but dropped hairs be may quite irritating when handling. Lives in shallow burrows. Keep like a scrubland species, but provide a humidifying shelter. Unless your are keeping it on moistened vermiculite.

Chilean fire tarantula *(Grammostola spatulata)*

An attractive spider with orangeish coloration, particularly in sunlight. The care is similar to the Chilean rose. It is somewhat more nervous from a handling point of view than the Chilean rose. Supposedly, this species will seek shelters rather than dig a burrow.

The striped-knee or zebra tarantula (*Rhechosticta seemanni*). Some of these rank among the most beautiful of the tarantulas.

Chilean rose tarantula (*Grammostola gala*). This attractive and easily maintained spider is one of the best choices for a tarantula pet that you can handle.

Pink-toed tarantulas *(Avicularia sp.)*

Several members of the genus *Avicularia*, particularly *Avicularia avicularia* are sold under this name. Most available animals are imported from Guyana. They are occasionally offered as captive-born animals. This is one the smaller tarantulas offered on the pet market. These arboreal tarantulas are usually very docile but can move quite fast. Their small size, long dense hairs and attractive coloration makes them very appealing. They should be kept in a container with a vertical piece of cork bark as a shelter and climbing area. They require high relative humidity (80% and up) or will die during molting. Some of the species of *Avicularia* have almost iridescent purple or dark violet abdominal and leg hairs; others have reddish hairs. *Avicularia* of similar sizes can be kept in groups in large vivaria for an interesting display and can be readily bred under such conditions. Around 100 eggs are laid within a large egg case. The eggs hatch in six to eight weeks. The spiderlings are relatively large and easily raised on crickets. The urticating hairs on these species can be quite irritating. Because they can be kept in groups in naturalistic vivaria, pink-toed tarantulas are one of the best and most entertaining choices for display type set-ups.

Lasiodora species

Lasiodora, which are primarily Brazilian, are seldom available in the U.S., except *Lasiodora parahybana*, usually as captive-raised spiderlings. Occasionally, they are available as captive-bred spiderlings from Europe.

These are among the largest and fastest growing of the tarantulas. There is a record of a *Lasiodora klugi* with a 9 /12 inch leg span that weighed nearly 3 oz. Care for them like tropical forest tarantulas at a relative humidity of 80% or more and at a temperature of 80-85 F. Some specimens, can attain a five inch leg span in one year. Females can probably reach sexual maturity in three years. *Lasiodora* are mostly terrestrial, but will rest on cork bark and seek shelter under cork bark. This is a fast moving spider and is not handleable.

Giant Bird Eaters *(Pamphobeteus)* species

Some of the *Pamphobeteus* are among the largest and heaviest of the tarantulas. One of the most impressive is *Pamphobeteus antinous..* Recently several *Pamphobeteus* species from Columbia have become available including *Pamphobetous fortis*. Keep *Pamphoboteus* like *Lasiodora*.

Goliath bird-eating spiders *(Theraphosa leblondi).*

These are the largest and among the most impressive spiders in the world. They are occasionally imported as adults from Guyana and sold at high prices. Mortality in imports can be significant, and one must be prepared to losing a percentage. The best approach is to buy the smallest animals and raise them up. Large animals may be old and relatively short-lived. Goliath bird-eaters are occasionally available as captive-bred animals imported from Europe; they do well, and they grow fast. This

50

Pink-toed tarantula (*Avicularia avicularia*). Few tarantulas can match the display potential of this species. Try a half dozen of these in a large planted vivarium in your living room. It will definitely grab the attention of your guests. These neat spiders will also readily breed.

The skeleton tarantula (*Ephebopus murinus*). This is a more subdued version of the zebra tarantula which is also quite aggressive.

species is aggressive, fast moving and not handleable. The will readily flick abdominal hairs when stressed and a bare-patched abdomen is a common condition with this species. If you like your spiders big and impressive, this is the one to get. Adults prefer large prey and will readily feed on "pink" mice. Whether a big, hairy, brown spider with a bare patch on the abdomen is attractive is a matter of opinion. Goliath bird-eater grow fast like *Lasiodora*. They should be cared for like *Lasiodora*. Males of this species are said to lack tibial spurs.

Skeleton tarantula *(Ephebopus murinus)*

These are occasionally imported out of French Guyana. At first they give the impression of being a striped-knee tarantula until one observes them more closely. The color is different, the abdomen is clothed in much finer hairs than the striped-knee. The size is about the same. It is a medium sized tarantula. When threatened this species has a an impressive display raising its body and front legs way up. It will readily bite. The author has not seen this species flick hairs. Keep like a rainforest tarantula.

Sri Lankan, Ornamental rainforest and Indian Mysore tarantulas (*Poecilotheria fasciata, P. regalis* and *P. striata*, respectively).

In terms of intricacy of pattern and color, these are among the most beautiful tarantulas in the world. The underside of the legs of adults is jet black and a striking lemon yellow. These arboreal tarantulas are very fast moving and, consequently, somewhat difficult to manage. It is essential that one adopts husbandry methods that do not require removing spiders from their enclosures unless one uses transfer procedures (i.e. jar to jar transfers) that preclude the animals being moved in the open. Larger individuals of similar size can be kept in small groups for breeding. Siliconing small sections of cork hollows to the sides of a glass tank or simply placing individual cork hollows vertically will result in individual spiders inhabiting respective cork hollows. These spiders will sometimes construct dense suspended sheet type of webs. Imported adults tend to be aggressive and can inflict a nasty bite with significant local effects, but captive-raised individuals aren't particularly aggressive. Theses spiders cannot be handled, but they make beautiful display animals. They are available (particularly *Poecilotheria regalis*) with some regularity as captive-bred animals from Europe. They are fast growing. Males bred and raised in captivity will reach sexual maturity by eighteen months. Following their last molt, males of *P. regalis* will emerge with a duller abdominal pattern and longer abdominal hairs than females. Males have no tibial spurs. Efforts should be made to make some of the other interesting species of *Poecilotheria* available in the hobby. These are among the best of the tarantulas: beauty, intricate pattern and good displays.

Asian bird eaters (*Haplopelma minax* and *Haplopelma albostriatum*)

These spiders are being imported out of Thailand and sold as Asian bird-eating spiders. There can be a high mortality in imports. These are nasty spiders that will bite readily. Do not handle. Their attractive features are their dense velvet appearance and the fact that they don't have or flick urticating hairs. They are somewhat more difficult to keep than other species. Very fast moving when in the open but secretive as display animals. They require high humidity and should be kept in the mid 70's to low 80's.

King baboon spider (*Citharischius crawshayi*)

These are the second largest tarantulas of Africa. The largest is the very rare Goliath baboon *Hysterocrates hercules*. King baboon spiders are among the most impressive of all the tarantulas. Not only are they large with thick legs, but they are in their own way attractive being densely covered with tight fine rusty red hairs that make them seem as if covered with crushed velvet. Imported king baboon spiders can also be among the most aggressive of the tarantulas. They will come at you with fangs raised forward hissing and seemingly rearing to go. This is an impressive spider any way you look at it. Recently, imported king baboon spiders have become more readily available, but they still remain one of the most expensive of the tarantulas. They are occasionally offered as captive-bred spiderlings from Europe. These should be raised on a layer of barely moist vermiculite where they will build burrows. Spiderlings are relatively slow growing suggesting that this species is probably very long lived. Captive-raised animals tend not to be particularly aggressive. Nonetheless, definitely do not handle this species. The king baboon spider is incomparable as a display animal. Can be kept on barely moist vermiculite with an artificial burrow or as a desert/scrubland species with a humidifying shelter. This author's favorite terrestrial tarantula.

Starburst baboon (*Pterinochilus murinus*)

Medium-sized tarantulas with a body length of 1 1/2 to 2 inches. Males smaller than females with tibial hooks. They should be kept like scrubland tarantulas. They will hide under shelters or construct burrows. A very fast tarantula that will climb up glass or plastic at good speed, making it somewhat difficult to manage. If provided with artificial burrows or a medium such as peat moss which allows for forming its own burrows, it becomes rather easy to manage. Starburst baboons are somewhat variable in color. The best have a bright yellow sunburst pattern on the cephalothorax and finely speckled and patterned abdomens with shades of yellow, green, grey and brown. This species is aggressive, and its bite will result in painful local effects; do not handle. It is offered with some regularity as imports and captive-bred spiderlings. It will lay around a hundred eggs which hatch in about 5 weeks. A second egg sac may be produced a few months after the first. The spiderlings are easily raised as long as adequate relative humidity is supplied.

Horned baboons

This genus is characterized by a foveal horn which ranges from a mound to a long horn. Two species are occasionally offered, the rhino horned baboon (*Ceratogyrus brachycephalus*) and the East African horned baboon (*Ceratogyrus darlingi*). These are sometimes offered as captive-bred spiderlings. They form burrows. They inhabit dry scrubland type of habitats.

Stout-legged baboon spiders *(Heterscodra sp)*

Recently, the greater stout-legged baboon spider (*Heterscodra crassipes*) has been imported in small numbers, presumably from Cameroon. This is a medium-sized, arboreal tarantula (1 1/2 - 2 1/2 inch body length) characterized by thick fourth legs with swollen femurs. Should be kept as a tropical rainforest species like *Avicularia*.

Feather-leg baboon spiders *(Stromatopelma)*

These arboreal tarantulas were formerly placed in the genus *Scodra*. The only species occasionally imported is the West African common feather-legged baboon (*Stromatopelma calceata*). This is another moderate size tarantula (1 3\4 -2 1\4 inch). It inhabits the higher regions of fern/palm trees where they build simple sheet webs at the base of palm fronds. Keep like stout-legged baboons.

Selenocosmids

Several species of *Selenocosmia* have recently been imported from SE Asia and Indonesia. We can expect more varieties of these spiders to become available in the future. Not much is known of their husbandry. They generally appear to require high relative humidity and should have water regularly available. Many, but not all, should be kept like tropical species at around 80 F, but some may prefer cooler temperatures (in the mid 70's). Most Selenocosmia are aggressive, and many dealers caution buyers about their bites. They are fast moving. One of the neatest is the Mount Obrie brown tarantula (*Selenocosmia lanipes*) from New Guinea with a chocolate brown body and velvety black legs. Another popular species is the Fak-Fak ochre (*Selenocosmia honesta*).

Ornamental rainforest tarantula (*Poecilotheria regalis*). One of the most beautiful of the tarantulas. This is a hardy, easily maintained species which can also move so fast that it is usually recommended for more experienced arachnoculturists.

King baboon spider (*Citharischius crawshayi*). A large, attractive, aggressive and expensive species which ranks as one of the most desirable of the tarantulas.

DISEASES AND DISORDERS

Interest in the treatment of diseases and disorders of animals usually develops if;
1. the animals are popular and
2. if they are relatively long-lived and
3. preferably expensive enough that people will consider treatment by a veterinarian rather than allow them to die.

In the case of tarantulas, there has been little interest in possible treatment, because most species sold in the pet trade are inexpensive enough that the cost of veterinary treatment becomes prohibitive. Furthermore, virtually nothing is known about the veterinary treatment of tarantulas. Depending on the quirks of the pet trade and if interest in more expensive species becomes more widespread, it is possible that a veterinary medicine concerned with treatment of tarantulas could evolve just as it has in the case of reptiles. The following are possible courses for the development of a veterinary medicine concerned with tarantulas.
With imports:

1. Stool checks for parasitic worms, protozoa, bacteria. Experimental treatments with vermifuges, anti-protozoal drugs such Flagyl (Metronidazole) and antibiotics. This may seem far-fetched, but if you've just paid 150-200.00 for a king baboon spider or giant bird eater, the cost of a stool check and treatment could prove to be worthwhile. If you are looking at the possibility of breeding, the desire to maintain healthy stock and to prevent the introduction of a disease or parasite to a colony may be a consideration.

2. Can methods be developed for diagnosing and removing parasitic larvae.

3. In the case of injuries, establish methods for stopping bleeding and closing up a ruptured abdomen.

Some of the more common problems one will encounter with tarantulas are:

RUPTURED ABDOMENS
The author has not personally encountered this problem to date but has been told of several incidents associated with falling either during handling or with injury caused by a sharp object within the vivarium. The author has investigated possible treatment on tarantulas which had recently died.

One of the first things one will notice when dissecting tarantulas is that the integument covering the abdomen is actually quite tough and not all that easy to cut through or puncture. In the case of a ruptured abdomen following a fall, there is no doubt that in addition to the ruptured abdomen, there will be a high probability of internal injuries which will not be visible from the outside. There is at this point little we can do to treat internal damage so the only recourse we have is to try to patch up the wound and hope for the best.

There are two reason why abdominal wounds should be patched up.
1. The tarantula may bleed to death.
2. The open wound makes it susceptible to infection and parasitism by small flies.

Generally internal pressure of the abdomen tends to keep any puncture wound or rupture open. If a you are confronted with a small puncture wound, the author has found that the a liquid bandage obtainable in drugstores such as Liquid Skin R, applied to the puncture area will do a fair job at covering the wound and sealing it as long as the area is first dried up with a piece of tissue paper. If this doesn't work, then resort to the following. For large ruptures, it is recommended to attempt to stitch the edges of the ruptured section as close together as possible. Then the area should be dried and a layer of (Bondini ® Everything Gel) glue applied along the edges to seal them. For those who feel uncomfortable stitching a tarantula's abdomen, the glue will fill small spaces. What negative effects this glue may have on a live tarantula if in contact with exposed abdominal contents has not been determined. The author only knows that it will successfully seal an abdominal wound rapidly. The glue will be more effective if the area surrounding the injury is shaved. This can be easily done with a hand razor. Excessive blood loss in a tarantula will eventually result in a loss of blood pressure visible in the abdominal area as it will appear to sag and pulse on the dorsal surface as the pericardium loses pressure.

DAMAGED LEGS

Any open wound on a tarantula should be covered. If a leg wound has occurred naturally at a joint, tarantulas have a mechanism to stop excessive bleeding. If the injury is not located at a joint but at the leg itself, bleeding may persist and one should resort to using a fast drying glue to seal it up. For joint injuries , a liquid bandage should be used because of a risk of parasitism by flies.

MOLTING PROBLEMS

This has been addressed in a previous section. If you provided adequate humidity, you should not have any molting problems with your tarantula. If a tarantula is upside down with obvious difficulties at emerging from the exoskeleton, Al David (1987. *Tarantulas. A Complete Introduction.* T.F.H.) recommends applying a solution of 2 teaspoonfuls of glycerine to two cupfuls of water on the old exoskeleton to soften it making sure one avoids the openings to the lungs.

If a tarantula has had problems molting one will sometimes find that it is hemorrhaging usually at the leg joints. One must use one's judgment as to whether to apply a liquid bandage such as Liquid Skin ®.

MITES

Some imported tarantulas, notably baboon spiders can harbor significant numbers of mites. These cannot readily be eradicated unless one is methodical in removing mites when present. The first thing is to keep the spider in a jar. The jar will be easy to clean and allow one to kill any stray mites by rinsing them away in warm water during maintenance. To remove mites from a spider, one method recommended by Russ Gurley, is to use a round tipped probe such as a knitting needle, dip the end in Vaseline ® and dab/pick off the mites individually. Removing only a few mites per treatment (they will adhere to the Vaseline ®) is recommended being careful not to apply any significant amount of Vaseline ® on the tarantula. In time, one may eventually get rid of all the mites.

FUNGAL INFECTIONS

These infections are uncommon in tarantulas. If they occur it is usually because one's vivarium is too wet with not enough ventilation. The first thing to do is to set the vivarium right. Any fungal growth on tarantulas tends to be superficial and can easily be removed with a cotton swab dipped in a Benomyl R solution.

UNDETERMINED CAUSES OF ILLNESS

A tarantula captures crickets but doesn't appear to digest them properly and a good deal of the cricket remains following attempted consumption. The tarantula fails to maintain a proper weight. This is a situation which is not uncommon with some imported tarantulas. The first thing to check is whether one is keeping the animal at a temperature which is high enough. Temperatures that are too low will affect feeding behavior and digestion. In many cases, the temperature will not be a factor and one must conclude that the tarantula has some sort of enteric disease. Hypothetically this could be determined by a stool check through microscopic examination or through a bacterial culture. An effective medication could be administered orally by injecting the abdomen of a live cricket and offering it as food or if available in an injectable form , injected directly into the abdomen. These are areas of experimentation which are worth investigating.

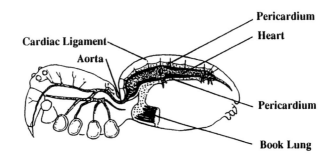

The circulatory system of the tarantula Illustration by Russ Gurley.

Part two
Scorpions

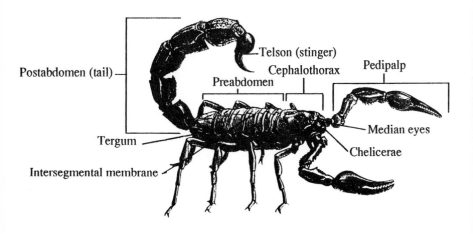

Postabdomen (tail)

Telson (stinger)

Cephalothorax

Pedipalp

Preabdomen

Tergum

Median eyes

Chelicerae

Intersegmental membrane

General Information

The author's first impression of a scorpion was one initially planted in his mind through a story told to him by is mother about the death of a friend in Algeria (N. Africa) from a scorpion sting. It was a sad tale of young girl inadvertently stepping barefoot on a scorpion and later treated by folk remedies. She was dead within twenty-four hours. It was several years later that the author was introduced to another scorpion by a priest while a resident at a catholic boarding school. This priest had a pet scorpion, a larger species which he would at times hold in his hand. Later the dead and dried scorpion adorned his office. Fear and horror had been replaced by curiosity and later wonderment. Looking back, this combination of caution and fascination would be a reasonable one when involved with keeping scorpions as a hobby. As a whole, the great majority of species are relatively harmless creatures, but a few warrant all the caution that has ever been conveyed about scorpions.

WHY KEEP SCORPIONS

Some of the larger and most recommended species of scorpions look and behave like some miniature science fiction machines. Indeed, one of the aesthetic appeals of large scorpions is in their armored, hinged and nearly mechanical appearance. Many species also have a smooth shine or sheen and will glow greenish under a black light, looking like small fluorescent lobsters. To put it simply, scorpions are kind of neat. Even their behaviors such as the way they move, the way they catch prey and hold it in their claws, and the "promenade-a-deux" performed during breeding are fascinating to observe. As pets, scorpions are undemanding creatures requiring little space and relatively little maintenance to fare well in captivity.

A PHILOSOPHY OF SCORPION KEEPING

There are so many species of scorpions that are relatively harmless and safe to keep that there is really no good reason for anyone other than scientists to own dangerously venomous species. Most are not particularly attractive, and the medical consequences of their stings can result in death, because effective treatment usually requires a specific antivenin. The sale of such species to hobbyists should be of considerable concern. The day a hobbyist or other individual were to die as a result of the sting of an imported scorpion, there is a risk that restrictive legislation could be proposed that would affect the keeping of all scorpions. The author recommends that no species known to cause fatalities or serious medical complications be kept or sold except under a permit system similar to that enforced by states with sound policies regulating the keeping of venomous snakes (i.e., Florida). Under such a permit system, such species could not be kept by minors. In addition, individuals would be required to keep any dangerous species in locked cages or vivaria to prevent any possibility of escape or accidental access into the enclosure. Such enclosures would be housed in a room kept locked at all times except when occupied by the owner or other advised and responsible adults. A sign shall be posted in the front of the vivarium indicating the name and scientific name of the species with a clearly indicated warning sign stating that the species is dangerous. The following species should be regulated under such a system.(from Keegan H.L. 1980. Scorpions of Medical Importance. Jackson: University Press of Mississippi. 140pp.)

FROM AFRICA AND THE MIDDLE EAST

Androctonus species (particularly *A. australis, A. amoreuxi, A. bicolor, A. crassicauda, A. mauritanicus*)
Hottentota minax (formerly *Buthus minax*)
Buthus occitanus
Leiurus quinquestriatus
Mesobuthus gibbosus

SOUTH AFRICA

Parabuthus species (particularly *P. triadulatus, P. transvaalensis, P.villosus*)

NORTH AMERICA
UNITED STATES

Centruroides exilicauda (formerly *C. sculpturatus*)

MEXICO

Centruroides species (several species are dangerously venomous)

WEST INDIES

Tityus trinitatis

SOUTH AMERICA

Tityus species

ASIA

Buthotus tamulus

Note: Any such list must be deemed incomplete and would probably include additional species in the future. At the present time, of the roughly 1500 known species of scorpions, only 25 have a venom which is capable of causing human death.

Great Britain has established a licensing system that requires that an individual obtain a license to own or keep any scorpions in the family *Buthidae* (a family which includes virtually all species known to be dangerous to man though the majority of the buthid species are not considered dangerous).

PECTINES

The pectines are comb-like sensory structures located on the ventral side of scorpions behind the area where the last set of legs joins to the body and to the side of the postgenital fold. These structures, which are unique to scorpions, function primarily as mechanoreceptors and contact chemoreceptors. They play a key role in selecting areas suitable for spermatophore deposition by males in the course of breeding.

SEXING

The sexes in scorpions can usually be identified either by differences in size, and/or by differences in the relative size of body structures, and/or by differences in the shape of body structures, and/or by differences in the texture of the body surface and finally by differences in meristic characters. In many cases, these differences will not immediately be obvious and careful observation of the animals will be required to identify a particular sex. When no reference is available, sexes can best be identified when a large number of animals is available for comparison. One of the best indicators of sex in the most popular species in the pet trade, the emperor scorpion (Pandinus imperator) and the Asian forest scorpions (Heterometrus species) are differences in the relative size of the pectines. In these genera as with many species of scorpions, the pectines of males are larger than that of females. To observe the pectines, the animals can either be picked up at the base of the telson with foam covered forceps or tongs or they can be placed in an empty clear plastic shoe box and observed from below.

Pectines of emperor scorpions (*Pandinus imperator*). Note the larger pectinal teeth on a male (left) compared to a female (right).

Housing and Maintenance

For the most part, scorpions are not really suitable for attractive displays because they are primarily nocturnal and when provided with shelters will spend most of the time concealed. Some success has been obtained using 25 watt red incandescent bulbs for displaying scorpions in a nocturnal set-ups similar to those established in some of the large zoos. Many species will emerge and behave under this type of lighting as if they were in darkness.

ENCLOSURES

PLASTIC TERRARIA AND ALL-GLASS AQUARIA

Depending on the size and numbers of a given species that you wish to maintain, you will find that either plastic terraria (terrariums of the pet trade) or all glass terraria will prove suitable for displaying and maintaining various species of scorpions. Smaller scorpions can be kept in enclosures as small as plastic shoe boxes or five gallon tanks with tops. Larger species such as emperor or Asian forest scorpions will require sweater box size plastic containers or all-glass tanks at least 10 gallons with secure covers. Larger setups will be essential if you are keeping these scorpions in groups.

STORAGE BOXES

With scorpions, larger clear or translucent plastic storage boxes will often work well for maintaining large collections. A few small holes can be drilled or burned (using a soldering iron) through the cover but usually enough air seeps in through the seam, that holes are not necessary. The lids should be taped to prevent any risk of escape.

Covers

As with tarantulas, one should have secure covers on all containers with scorpions. Use either screw-on, snap on, hinged with a locking mechanism or taped on lids.

SUBSTRATES

Generally, forest scorpions can be kept on the same kinds of substrates recommended for forest tarantulas. Emperor scorpions and Asian forest scorpions will fare well on a substrate consisting of 1 1\2 to 2 inches of damp peat moss. They can also be kept on moistened vermiculite (12-15 parts vermiculite to 1 part water by volume), a medium highly recommended by Europeans. Fine orchid bark wetted prior to introduction will also work well, but doesn't allow for the formation of burrows.

For desert species, a dry, fine, rounded aquarium gravel or aquarium sand will be adequate.

SHELTERS

To prevent accidental crushing, rocks are not recommended as shelters. Instead natural cork bark which is light and attractive in appearance is recommended for creating shelters in vivaria housing scorpions. Even rock-dwelling species can be kept between layers of stacked cork bark. An advantage of cork is that it is light enough to be readily lifted with tongs, eliminating any risk of a possible sting when trying to uncover one's scorpion (s). There are currently a number of shelters made of plastic sold for the reptile trade that are suitable for scorpions. Some of the attractive reptile shelters made of concrete can be used but there is a risk of crushing with smaller scorpions. The enclosure design for housing scorpions should be simple to allow for ready monitoring and maintenance of the animals. The design should also be such that you have landscape structures arranged in such a way that you do not get accidentally stung lifting a piece of cork or moving a structure to find where your scorpion is hiding. KEEP THINGS SIMPLE!

ARTIFICIAL BURROWS

See tarantulas. Carefully design burrows for easy observation. Be careful when removing burrows for cleaning not to accidentally put your fingers or hands on a scorpion. There is always a risk of being stung when moving or removing landscape items. When possible, use tools such as tongs.

HEATING AND TEMPERATURE

The methods used for heating scorpions containers are essentially the same as for heating tarantula containers. If heating cables or heating pads are used, only a portion of the enclosure should be heated so that scorpions can avoid the high heat above the heat source and can select an area in the enclosure that they feel is adequate. The following are recommended temperatures for keeping some of the more common species available in the trade.

Subtropical/Tropical forest/High relative humidity : 78-85F
Florida bark scorpions (*Centruroides gracilis*)
Emperor scorpion (*Pandinus imperator*)
Red-clawed scorpion (*Pandinus sp.*)
Asian and Javanese forest scorpions (*Heterometrus spinifer* and *H. cyaneus*)

Desert/Scrubland/Moderate relative humidity inside a humidified shelter: 78-86F.
At night, desert scorpions will safely tolerate drops of 10 or more degrees. During the winter, they can be safely kept for four to eight weeks at temperatures in the 60's. This cooling period, during which many scorpions will not feed, may be

beneficial to induce breeding.
Hairy scorpions (*Hadrurus sp.*)
Israeli gold scorpion (*Scorpio maurus palmatus*)

Note: There are temperate species of scorpions which will fare well at room temperatures. If in doubt about the right temperature at which to keep a given species, research the climate of the country and area of origin. If the scorpion is a burrowing species, figure that the temperature in the burrow could be at least 10 F lower than the air temperature during the day. By the same token the night temperature will be more moderate in a burrow than at the surface. Many scorpion species are adaptable to a relatively wide range of temperatures and one can make adjustments by observing their behaviors.

TOOLS
Long forceps or tongs with foam rubber on the ends will prove invaluable when you need to transfer animals. Otherwise, the same tools as recommended for tarantulas will prove useful.

MAINTENANCE
Scorpions, as a whole are not very messy. Any dead or uneaten insects should be removed on a regular basis, and the substrate should be changed when needed. For many species, changing the substrate once every six months to a year is sufficient. Water and food should be provided regularly and with forest species, a light misting two or three times a week is recommended.

The emperor scorpion *(Pandinus imperator).*

Feeding

All the scorpions currently offered in the pet trade will feed readily on crickets and mealworms and the large species will also feed on prekilled small mice. The smaller species should be offered correspondingly smaller insects such as half grown mealworms or 2-3 week old crickets instead of 4-6 week olds. The prey can be placed in the enclosure or, with some of the less nervous species, it can be offered pre-killed off of long forceps to the individual animals by bringing the prey close to their mouth parts. The larger species will readily take large crickets or large mealworms (*Zoophobas*) in this manner and will eventually grab the prey in their claws. Emperor scorpions will actually take food out of their owners hands even while handled. If live prey is introduced into the vivarium, crickets should have their legs pinched at the "knee" joints which will cause them to drop their hind legs. This will allow them to be more readily captured by scorpions. Mealworms should be pinched at midbody and placed in a shallow dish or there is a risk that they will burrow into the substratum before a scorpion can find them. All insects should be well fed and given a source of water such as oranges prior to feeding (see feeding under tarantulas). Some of the very large scorpions, particularly emperor scorpions will feed on pre-killed " pink" (newborn) mice. A larger pre-killed mouse with the viscera exposed will readily be consumed if introduced in a container with a large number of adult emperor scorpions. One of the nice features of scorpions is that many species can fast for weeks and even months (desert species such as Hadrurus) without any serious consequences. Going away on a week-end or short vacation is unlikely to be a problem if you keep scorpions.

FEEDING REGIMENS

Most adult scorpions will fare well on a feeding regimen of one to two prey items of an appropriate size once a week. A number of desert species will fare well on feeding regimens whereby prey is offered every two to three weeks.
Baby scorpions should be offered food twice a week.

Scorpions kept in groups should be offered enough insects to adequately feed all animals at a given feeding. It is a good idea, when keeping animals in groups to add a few extra prey items once or twice a week to prevent the possibility of cannibalism.

OVERFEEDING

Several authors warn that scorpions can be overfed and may possibly die as a result. The primary symptoms of overfeeding are listlessness and the distended pleural and intersegmental membranes resulting in separation of the tergites. The initial impression of such scorpions is that they are swollen as if pregnant. The general feeling on this issue is that some distension following feeding is normal, but too much is unhealthy and may lead to death. The cause of death is presumed to be inability to properly digest the ingested matter before some begins to decompose. Scorpions, it appears, cannot regurgitate.

WATER

All species should be offered a shallow dish with water such as a bottle cap or jar top or a plastic floor guard. Forest species should be lightly misted two or three times a week. Many desert species such as hairy scorpions (Hadrurus) will do fine without any water at all and obtain water primarily from their food. Nonetheless hobbyists will occasionally lightly mist desert species because it is believed they may obtain water in desert areas from condensation. If in doubt about a given species, offer water.

MOLTING

Molting is a critical period when raising scorpions. This will not be an issue with most scorpions sold in the pet trade because adult animals do not molt once they have reached sexual maturity (there is some question as to whether females of some species may molt after sexual maturity). But if you are raising captive-born or bred scorpions, you will notice that a high percentage of deaths will occur because of molting difficulties. At each successive molt, there will be a high percentage of mortality and in the author's experience the mortality rate becomes greater as the animals become larger. In scorpions raised in the laboratory, about one third of all scorpions die at each successive molt. Mortality rates prior to sexual maturity, when rearing captive-born scorpions in captivity, vary between 95 and 100%. Tropical forest species such as emperor scorpions have high initial survival rates but the mortality rate increases as the animals become larger.

The frequency of molting will vary among species. Many factors including diet, and temperature at which reared, will affect both the growth rate and the intervals between molts. Many smaller species of scorpions will reach sexual maturity after 4-5 molts, usually completed within a year. Other species, including the emperor scorpions and Asian forest scorpions sold in the pet trade, will undergo at least seven molts over several years before reaching sexual maturity.

In summary, one can say that baby and subadult scorpions are difficult to rear while adults tend to do rather well in captivity. The single factor that influences the captive success at these various stages factors is molting. In emperor scorpions, young animals often die when in molt. Larger emperors may have problematic molts that result in deformities of the limbs and or partial loss of limbs or of the telson. These injuries can be problematical and provide avenues for parasitism by flies (see molting problems under the diseases and disorders in the tarantula section for dealing with this).

What can one do to reduce the incidence of molt related deaths? Factors involving relative humidity and soil moisture may be associated with molting problems.

During the molting process, as the new exoskeleton is secreted by the epidermis underneath the old exoskeleton, some materials are reabsorbed from the old cuticle. The blood pressure of scorpions apparently increases at one point causing the cuticle at the sides and the front margins of the old exoskeleton to rupture. Many scorpions die because this process fails to successfully occur. It is possible that excess moisture may contribute to cuticular elasticity that allows it to resist rupturing. It is also possible that inadequate relative humidity prevents proper molting much as it does with tarantulas. The fact is that many scorpions including emperor scorpions die after the 24 hour period of sluggishness that normally precedes a molt. The author recommends creating an environment that provides a variety of humidity levels (i.e. dry under some areas with humidified shelters in others). In the end, only long term experimentation is likely to resolve the problems in this particular area of scorpion husbandry. Were it not for the molting problems, scorpions would be considered easy to raise and maintain.

Molted exoskeletons of a large and a small emperor scorpion.

A close-up of the molt of an immature emperor scorpion. Note the uplifted carapace that allows the molting scorpion to emerge from its old "skin".

Handling

The general rule with regards to the handling of scorpions is DON'T. Yet, one of the interests of many aspiring scorpion owners is the possibility of handling their animals. What they want is a scorpion pet with which they can have a certain amount of regular and direct interaction. Of the various species offered in the pet trade, only one can be recommended as a candidate for handling: the large emperor scorpion (*Pandinus imperator*). This is a remarkably docile species that needs to be pestered to be induced to sting (not an easy task with established animals). The consequences of the sting are often insignificant. Some individuals will describe a sting as being nothing more than a pin prick while others experience brief localized pain and reddening at the site of the sting. There have been a few cases of individuals receiving multiple stings at one time while unpacking imports with no significant consequences. Generally, the symptoms of emperor scorpion stings are gone within a few hours. One should, however, be aware of the possibility of an unusual reaction to a sting and must be prompt to seek medical attention should an unusual reaction develop.

Nonetheless, when considering handling scorpions, a general rule should be abided by all scorpions owners.

NO CHILDREN SHALL BE ALLOWED TO HANDLE SCORPIONS

The effects of a sting on children because of their small size are likely to be significantly more severe. Though emperor scorpions are unlikely to sting a child which handles them in the proper manner and though it is unlikely that their venom would have life-threatening medical effects, as responsible adults we should not expose children to the possibility of a sting. By the same token, there are many other animals that are suitable as pets for adults but not for children such as saltwater lionfish and scorpion fish, various species of large birds and mammals and other invertebrates such as bees etc.

Regarding the handling of emperor scorpions, there are literally thousands that are handled annually in the pet trade. It is not uncommon for an individual to put his hand in a container with a hundred or more emperor scorpions to select a particular animal. As a general rule, imported scorpions that have been allowed to feed and settle down are less likely to sting than starved individuals from a freshly imported group. If one is gentle, scorpions are easily moved in these containers. Emperor scorpions, particularly larger animals have a low propensity to using their stingers for defensive purposes. They have to feel seriously threatened to do so. All and all they are docile and very consistent in their behaviors.

A method recommended by some for picking up emperor scorpions for handling is to grab an animal by the tail right at the base of the stinger (telson) and place it in one's hand. In the author's experience, this method is problematical because if one doesn't do it just right, one can get stung. Furthermore, species that are normally quite calm including emperor scorpions get distressed and excited by this practice. Slowly approaching an animal and gently scooping it up in one's hand works well with emperor scorpions. Some hobbyists will also do this with large Asian forest scorpions, but there is a much higher risk of getting stung with these species. If you want a scorpion to handle, stick with the emperor scorpion (*Pandinus imperator*). The related red-clawed emperor (*Pandinus* species) sold in the pet trade has a much lower threshold for using its stinger and is not recommended for handling.

In conclusion, scorpions are primarily animals to be observed. You should be aware that any handling or advocating of handling will be at your own risk. None of the material related to handling has been presented to advocate the handling of any species of scorpion, including the emperor scorpion, but to present facts as to the potential for handling of scorpion species should an adult decide to do so.

SAFE METHODS FOR CATCHING AND TRANSFERRING SCORPIONS

Scorpions in the course of maintenance can be guided with long forceps from one container to another. For grabbing and picking up scorpions one can use long forceps (10-12 inch) with the ends padded with foam rubber (attach with rubber bands or glue) and grab them just in front of the telson (stinger). This is a method which works well for collecting live animals in the field. The use of foam coated forceps will reduce any likelihood of crushing damage or injury when grabbing scorpions with these tools. The barbecue tongs used to turn meat at barbecues are also used by some hobbyists for grabbing scorpions. The ends of these should also be padded with foam rubber.

Transferring an Asian forest scorpion (*Heterometrus*) to its container using foam padded tongs.

Breeding

During actual breeding, a behavior which has been called "promenade-a-deux", a male grasps a female's pedipalps (claws) with his own and leads her to a suitable site (a smooth surface) for him to deposit a spermatophore. The male then pulls the female over the site where the spermatophore was deposited, and she lowers herself over the spermatophore to transfer the sperm through her genital opening. Thus, a key to the successful breeding of scorpions will be to provide a suitable site for deposition of the spermatophore and the ensuing breeding process. This is a simplification of the relatively complex associated breeding behaviors of many scorpions and one should refer to Polis (1990) for additional information on this subject.

If provided with a layer of moist substratum placed on top of a glass or plastic floor, emperor scorpions when breeding will dig burrows and there will be evidence of the floor of the enclosure being cleared of any medium in one or more areas. A few months later one or more females will appear gravid. As the time for giving birth gets closer, whitish masses will become visible through the intersegmental membrane.

For the successful breeding of desert scorpions, areas with a smooth surface should be provided such as smooth rounded rocks, small smooth pieces of wood or even a small piece of glass or plastic.

RAISING BABY SCORPIONS

Soon after birth, baby scorpions will collect on the mother's back. They will usually remain there without feeding until after their first molt. After the first molt, babies will begin to scatter and feed and there will be a high risk of cannibalism by both the mother and the babies. At that time, with most species, it is wise to transfer baby scorpions to their own rearing container(s). Small shelters and regular misting should be provided. Food in the form of pinhead to one week old crickets should be regularly available. Crushed mealworms and larger crickets with the abdominal contents exposed will also be suitable for feeding baby scorpions. In the case of emperor scorpions and Asian forest scorpions, babies can be raised in groups. With emperor scorpions, babies will do best when raised with the mother. Female emperor scorpions will actually catch and crush crickets that they eventually drop on the ground. The baby scorpions will then gather around the dead crickets and feed. It is probable that several other "communal" scorpion species perform this behavior and this should always be a consideration when attempting to rear young animals.

With emperor scorpions, one will have much greater success by rearing captive born young with the mother compared to rearing them in individual containers.

A pregnant emperor scorpion bred by the author.

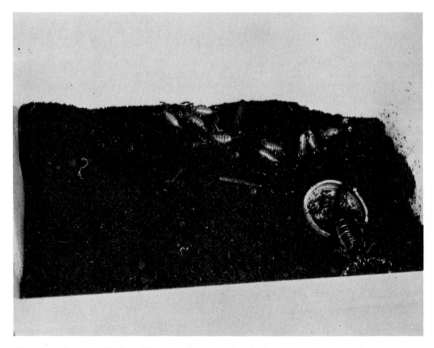

The same female with its offspring raised together in the same container. Raising babies with their mother is the most recommended method for rearing this species.

Notes on Popular Species

The following information is provided on the species most frequently offered in the U.S. pet trade. Hopefully, in the future additional species, such as some of the desirable large S. African Ischnurids (*Hadogenes sp.*) and scorpionids (*Opistophthalmus sp.*) will become available.

No known dangerous species of scorpion should be sold in the pet trade, and none of the dangerous species currently offered are covered here.

THE EMPEROR SCORPION (*Pandinus imperator*). Scorpionidae

This is the largest living species of scorpion. It is a forest dwelling species which forms burrows. In the wild, a favorite diet is millipedes.

Size
Adults can reach a length of nearly eight inches (20 cm) and can weigh more than 60 grams. As with many species of scorpions, there is considerable variation in the size of *Pandinus imperator*. Some are "giants" which will come close to attaining the large size reputed for the species while many others will remain within a normal range of four to six inches. These differences may be attributed to several factors including environmental conditions, diet and possibly genetic variations among populations.

Sexing
In emperor scorpions, differences in the size of the pectines are the easiest way to sex specimens. Compared to a female, the male's pectinal teeth will be significantly larger.

Origin
Most imported animals are from Togo or Ghana

Growth
The emperor scorpion reaches sexual maturity after 6-7 molts which can require 3 1/2 to 7 years.

Longevity
Probably shorter in males than in females. 5-8 years and possibly longer.

Emperor scorpions should be kept on barely moist peat moss or dampened vermiculite several inches deep to allow them to dig burrows. The temperature should be 78-85 F. Shelters should be provided. They can be kept in groups. They will breed readily in captivity.

In the wild, the mother-offspring association may last for several months or years, and offspring may remain with the family group as adults. In captivity, the young are best raised with the mother. Food should be regularly available to reduce the probability of cannibalism. If raised with their mother on a slightly moist medium that allows for burrowing, one has a good chance of raising young from this species to maturity.

RED CLAWED SCORPION (*Pandinus* species).

This is another species of *Pandinus* which is occasionally imported. It is characterized by large, flattened, reddish claws. Red-clawed scorpions can be kept like emperor scorpions. This species is more agressive than emperor scorpions and much less reluctant to sting. Do not handle.

ASIAN FOREST SCORPIONS (*Heterometrus* species, primarily *H. spinifer*).

These large (up to 6 inches) shiny scorpions are impressive and have great form. They require about 7 molts to sexual maturity. Under optimal conditions sexual maturity is said to be reached in about a year. Their maintenance is similar to that of emperor scorpions. They are not recommended for handling. There have been several cases of individuals in the pet industry stung while handling *Heterometrus* imported from Thailand. Symptoms included pain, redness at the sight of the sting and mild swelling. The stings were of little consequence and the symptoms subsided within 24 hours. However, caution is warranted with members of this genus since some species of *Heterometrus* have caused temporary paralysis and irregularities in breathing.

JAVANESE SCORPIONS (*Heterometrus*) Scorpionidae.

Most of the ones imported are supposedly *Heterometrus cyaneus*. Their care is similar to S.E. Asian scorpions.

ISRAELI GOLD SCORPION (*Scorpio maurus palmatus*). Scorpionidae

There is also a black form of this species being imported as Israeli black scorpions (*Scorpio maurus fuscus*). Animals sold in the pet trade originate from Egypt or Israel.

Red-clawed scorpion (*Pandinus species*) in a defensive display. This is not a bluff. This species will readily sting.

Asian forest scorpion (*Heterometrus spinifer*). These are interesting large scorpions that can be kept communally.

Size
Up to 2 3/4 in.

Reproduction
8-13 young
This small attractive species is currently being imported in small numbers from Israel. It is considered to be relatively harmless with minor local effects resulting from a sting. However some caution is advised because it has been suggested that some populations in the Middle East may vary in their toxicity. *Scorpio maurus* are behaviorally interesting because they will forms burrows by moving the substrate including large pebbles. In large enclosures, they can be kept in small groups where animals will form individual burrows.

Scorpio maurus can be kept on sand like *Hadrurus* or on foam dug out to create artificial burrows placed over dry vermiculite or sand. Other substrate mixes should be experimented with to find a medium suitable for the formation of burrows. A single, humidified shelter using moist vermiculite is recommended to facilitate molting.

FLORIDA BARK SCORPIONS (*Centruroides gracilis*). Buthidae.

A small, flattened, dull black species found in somewhat moist areas by overturning rocks, bark, sections of wood or dried palm leaves or litter. This species can be kept in groups like emperor scorpions. They require smaller crickets (1 week-2 week) as food. Males will reach sexual maturity after 5-6 molts. Females after 6 molts. Sexual maturity is reached at 6-8 months. Longevity is 31-52 months. Litter size is 26 to 91. Ron Dupont has successfully maintained and bred this species in a twenty gallon long tank by placing a sheet of newspaper folded in four (as a shelter) placed in one corner and a flat dish with a soaked sponge at the other corner for water. They can also be kept on peat moss or soil. Up to thirty adults can be housed in this set-up and in time several hundred individuals will have been bred. According to Ron, females may play a role in the feeding of the baby scorpions much like the emperor scorpion. When breeding and keeping large numbers of this species, one will find a light, pale, colored morph occasionally emerge in a culture. According to Ron Dupont, raising this species to sexual maturity is relatively easy. A high relative humidity is recommended; 80% or more. The sting of *Centruroides gracilis* is painful, but usually of no great consequence. Do not handle.

HAIRY SCORPIONS (*Hadrurus species*). Iuridae.

These attractive desert scorpions are occasionally available from specialized dealers. In states where they occur, they can often be road collected at night or collected in the field by using a portable black light. They have a pale yellowish-beige coloration which is quite attractive. The Arizona hairy scorpion (*Hadrurus hirsutus*), which can attain a length of four inches, is the largest of the U.S. scorpions. *Hadrurus* species are extremely hardy and will do well on sand as a substratum.

At the time of writing, the author has a specimen of *H. californicum* which he collected three years ago. It has survived in a plastic shoe box with sand kept in a darkened area of the house. It has never been given water and is fed crickets every three weeks. It has not molted since it was captured.

Hadrurus will readily cannibalize conspecifics and other scorpions when hungry. Desert hairy scorpions should not be handled because they will readily sting. The sting is painful with local effects but not particularly dangerous. These scorpions are very tolerant of extremes of temperature. Some species of *Hadrurus* are among the longest lived of scorpions with records of specimens of *Hadrurus arizonensis* living up to twenty-five years.

Israeli gold scorpion (*Scorpio maurus palmatus*). This small species will move small pebbles in the process of building a burrow.

Hairy scorpion (*Hadrurus sp.*). These are some of the most attractive of the U.S. scorpions. They are also hardy and very long-lived although poor success has been had rearing captive-born animals.

Hairy scorpion with babies. Photo by Russ Gurley.

Scorpions:
Source Materials

Keegan, H.L. 1980. Scorpions of Medical Importance. Jackson: University Press of Mississippi. 140 pp.

Polis, G. 1990. The Biology of Scorpions. Stanford University Press, CA. 587 pp.

Hull-Williams, V. 1988. How to Keep Scorpions. Fitzgerald Publishing. London, England. 17 pp.

About the Author

Philippe de Vosjoli was born in 1949 in Paris, France. When in his teens, he was introduced to naturalistic vivarium design by an eccentric former keeper at the Jardin des Plantes.

Since that time he has pursued a life-long interest in the husbandry and propagation of amphibians and reptiles. He earned his bachelors degree at the University of Miami, Florida and has completed graduate studies in biology at Harvard University. He has authored and coauthored with Robert Mailloux several papers on the captive husbandry and propagation of frogs and lizards.

In 1987 he founded the American Federation of Herpetoculturists, the non-profit organization which publishes the quality magazine *The Vivarium,* and whose goals are to disseminate information about herpetoculture and represent the interests of herpetoculturists. His current research focused on developing methods for sustained maintenance and propagation of various tropical frogs, tiliquine skinks, green iguanas and various agamid lizards.